THE SOCIAL INFLUENCE PROCESS
IN COUNSELING AND PSYCHOTHERAPY

THE SOCIAL INFLUENCE PROCESS
IN COUNSELING AND PSYCHOTHERAPY

Edited by

FRED J. DORN, Ph.D.

Associate Professor
Counseling Psychology
Memphis State University

With Nineteen Contributors

CHARLES C THOMAS • PUBLISHER
Springfield • Illinois • U.S.A.

Published and Distributed Throughout the World by

CHARLES C THOMAS • PUBLISHER
2600 South First Street
Springfield, Illinois 62794-9265

© *1986 by* CHARLES C THOMAS • PUBLISHER
ISBN 0-398-05256-5
Library of Congress Catalog Card Number: 86-5843

With THOMAS BOOKS *careful attention is given to all details of manufacturing
and design. It is the Publisher's desire to present books that are satisfactory as to their
physical qualities and artistic possibilities and appropriate for their particular use.*
THOMAS BOOKS *will be true to those laws of quality that assure a good name
and good will.*

Printed in the United States of America
Q-R-3

Library of Congress Cataloging in Publication Data
The Social influence process in counseling and
psychotherapy.

    Bibliography: p.
    Includes index.
    1. Counseling--Social aspects. 2. Psycho-
therapy--Social aspects. 3. Influence (Psychology)
I. Dorn, Fred J. [DNLM: 1. Counseling.
2. Psychology, Social. 3. Psychotherapy. WM 55
S678]
BF637.C6S65 1986   158'.3   86-5843
ISBN 0-398-05256-5

CONTRIBUTORS

John G. Borkowski is Professor of Psychology at the University of Notre Dame.

Charles D. Claiborn is an Associate Professor of Counseling Psychology at the University of Iowa.

David N. Dixon is Professor of Educational Psychology and Coordinator of Doctoral Studies in Education at the University of Nebraska-Lincoln.

Fred J. Dorn is an Associate Professor of Counseling Psychology at Memphis State University.

Edward J. Heck is a Professor of Counseling Psychology and a staff member of the University Counseling Center at the University of Kansas.

Martin Heesacker is Assistant Professor of Psychology in the Counseling Psychology program at Ohio State University.

P. Paul Heppner is a Counseling Psychologist and has a dual appointment in the Department of Psychology and Counseling Services at the University of Missouri-Columbia.

Barbara A. Kerr is an Assistant Professor of Counselor Education at the University of Iowa.

James W. Lichtenberg is a Professor of Counseling Psychology and Director of the University Counseling Center at the University of Kansas.

Naomi M. Meara is a Professor of Counseling Psychology at the University of Notre Dame.

Monica M. Menne is a doctoral student in counseling psychology at the University of Missouri-Columbia.

Douglas H. Olson is a doctoral student in counseling psychology at the University of Nebraska-Lincoln.

Terry M. Pace is a doctoral student in Counseling Psychology at the University of Nebraska-Lincoln.

Michael J. Patton is Professor and Head of the Department of Educational and Counseling Psychology at the University of Tennessee in Knoxville.

Joan I. Rosenberg is a doctoral student in Counseling Psychology at the University of Missouri-Columbia.

Cal D. Stoltenberg is Director of Training and Associate Professor of Counseling Psychology at the University of Oklahoma.

Stanley R. Strong is a Professor in the Department of Psychology, Virginia Commonwealth University.

Terence J. Tracey is an Assistant Professor of Counseling Psychology in the Department of Educational Psychology, at the University of Illinois at Urbana/Champaign.

Alice M. Vargas is Staff Clinical Psychologist for the San Diego Regional Center for the Developmentally Disabled of San Diego, California.

C. Edward Watkins, Jr., is an Assistant Professor of Psychology at North Texas State University.

**To Eileen Riley Kolf,
she influenced all whom she met**

PREFACE

COUNSELOR TRAINING programs espouse a scientist-practitioner model. Therefore, counselors quickly learn the importance of investigating and evaluating the efforts that they put into practice. Counseling practitioners and researchers have made this effort in the area of social influence theory as it relates to the counseling process. Since the proposal was initially set forth by Strong (1968) that counseling be considered a process of interpersonal influence, numerous research articles on the topic have appeared in the counseling literature. In fact, Wampold and White (1985) indicated in an analysis of contemporary research themes in counseling literature, that social influence theory was the topical area most frequently investigated.

My purpose in bringing together this collection of readings was to stimulate the thinking of both practitioners and researchers with the latest developments in social influence theory, much of which can be applied to either one's practice or existing research program. As the editor of this book, I invited contributors who were not only active in examining social influence theory as it relates to counseling but also individuals who I perceived to be on the "cutting edge" of this topical area.

For those who are unfamiliar with social influence theory as it relates to counseling, the initial chapter will serve as an introduction. The chapter will also serve as a refresher for those who are familiar with the initial titles on this subject: *Change Through Interaction: Social Psychological Processes of Counseling and Psychotherapy* (Strong & Claiborn, 1982) and *Counseling as Applied Social Psychology: An Introduction to the Social Influence Model* (Dorn, 1984).

Some of what lies before you has been substantiated empirically, while the rest is speculative. Regardless of whether the author's assumptions are empirical or intuitive, however, it is important that you realize that each one believes that what he or she has brought forth for consideration plays a vital role in the counseling process. I trust that these ideas spark some interest in the social influence model. Perhaps the groundbreaking work that has been discussed in this volume will influence you to pursue both practice and research on the model.

FRED J. DORN

ACKNOWLEDGMENTS

AS A PUBLISHED WRITER I have spoken on several occasions with both authors and editors. During the course of these conversations I have heard some fairly grim stories about the difficulties one can encounter when attempting to bring together a book of readings. There is always one author who commits to writing a chapter and then excuses himself for no apparent reason. Then, of course, there is the author who agrees to write forty pages of manuscript and then mails ten. And finally, there is the author who refuses to make any changes because it is sure to compromise his integrity. I have no reason to doubt the authenticity of such stories. I must confess, however, that I did not encounter any of these cumbersome obstacles during the course of this project. I feel that the individuals who have contributed to this book did so in a most professional manner. I must say as well that I was impressed from the outset with not only the quality of their work but also with the experienced manner in which they responded to my requests for revisions and my suggestions for enhancing their contribution. I trust that I treated them as well.

While everyone involved in the project deserves credit for their efforts, I would like to especially express my gratitude to some specific individuals who offered additional support and counsel while I was developing this project. First and foremost, I would like to acknowledge Stan Strong's willingness to share not only his work but also himself. I deeply appreciate his enthusiastic support of my efforts to bring the social influence model into the arena of the practicing therapist. I truly believe as well that this project came together because of his involvement.

The support of Chuck Claiborn and Dave Dixon during the revision process was timely and welcomed. I feel their observations on the role of contributors and the concerns of publishers were insightful and confirming of my own suspicions.

Finally, I would like to express my heartfelt thanks to Marty Heesacker for his candid reactions to the plight of a writer who while employed in a service-oriented agency will invariably encounter numerous obstacles which are both real and manufactured.

Last but surely not least, I would like to thank Marcy Cayo for her efforts during the last stages of this project. With a keen eye for detail, she enhanced the quality of this project by reducing inconsistencies throughout the manuscript.

CONTENTS

Page

Preface ix

Chapter

1. The Social Influence Model: An Overview 3
   Fred J. Dorn
2. Interpersonal Influence Theory and
   Therapeutic Interactions 17
   Stanley R. Strong
3. Social Influence: Toward a General Theory of Change 31
   Charles D. Claiborn
4. Extrapolating From the Elaboration Likelihood Model of
   Attitude Change to Counseling 43
   Martin Heesacker
5. Elaboration Likelihood and the Counseling Process 55
   Cal D. Stoltenberg
6. Understanding Client Variables in the
   Social Influence Process 65
   Barbara A. Kerr, Douglas H. Olson, Terry M. Pace, and
   Charles D. Claiborn
7. Client Resistance and Social Influence 75
   David N. Dixon
8. Language Use and Social Influence in Counseling 85
   Naomi M. Meara and Michael J. Patton
9. Physical Attractiveness, Social Influences, and
   Counseling Processes 95
   Alice M. Vargas and John G. Borkowski

10. The Stages of Influence in Counseling and Psychotherapy 107
    Terence J. Tracey
11. A Social Influence Interpretation of the Adlerian
    Vocational Counseling Process 117
    C. Edward Watkins, Jr.
12. Methodological Approaches to the Study of Interpersonal
    Influence in Counseling Interaction 123
    James W. Lichtenberg and Edward J. Heck
13. Some Reflections on the Interpersonal Influence
    Process in Counseling 137
    P. Paul Heppner, Monica M. Menne, and Joan I. Rosenberg

Bibliography 147
Author Index 161
Subject Index 165

Undoubtedly we have no questions to ask which are unanswerable. We must trust the perfection of the creation so far as to believe that whatever curiosity the order of things has awakened in our minds, the order of things can satisfy.

A foolish consistency is the hobgoblin of little minds, adored by little statesmen and philosophers and divines. With consistency a great soul has simply nothing to do . . . . Speak what you think today in hard words and tomorrow speak what tomorrow thinks in hard words again, though it contradict everything you said today.

RALPH WALDO EMERSON

THE SOCIAL INFLUENCE PROCESS
IN COUNSELING AND PSYCHOTHERAPY

CHAPTER 1

THE SOCIAL INFLUENCE MODEL: AN OVERVIEW

Fred J. Dorn

COUNSELING IS A process which results from the interaction that occurs between two individuals—the counselor and the client. More than fifteen years ago, Goldstein (1966) noted that a significant body of research was available on two-person interactions throughout the literature in social psychology. At that time, he suggested that counseling psychologists examine the literature, extrapolate from it, and test some of the principles discovered through social psychological research in the context of the counseling relationship.

Two years after Goldstein published his paper, Stanley Strong (1968) responded with a landmark paper (Heesacker, Heppner, & Rogers, 1982) in which he proposed that counseling was a process of interpersonal influence. In other words, he proposed that clients encounter difficulty in their lives as a result of the attitudes they possess and it is the counselor's task to change the client's attitudes through the process of interpersonal influence. The focus of the counselor's attention should be on the client's attitudes because attitudes precede behavior, and the counselor who influences attitudes is also influencing behavior.

Strong's (1968) proposal was a daring and innovative one at the time. Counseling psychology was still in the midst of embracing theories that encouraged a more passive role for the counselor.

Attitude change, as Strong (1968) conceptualized it, would occur in a two-stage process. Initially, clients seek counseling because they are in a static state of behavior. This static state of behavior is a result of the

3

attributions that the client makes about his or her circumstances. More often than not, clients who are in a static state of behavior attribute their difficulty to factors over which they have little or no control. For example, the individual who states that he or she is incapable of finding love or happiness in the world because the person they care for does not care for them is attributing his or her personal difficulty to a factor over which they have little or no control. Obviously, this person cannot make another person love them, but this set of circumstances does not limit them to a life without love or happiness. Rather, this person is quite capable of finding love and happiness in their life, but they must begin to accept the idea that their love or happiness in life will more than likely be shared with someone else.

The client who seeks counseling does so because he or she believes that the counselor possesses the knowledge and resources to assist him or her in moving from this static state of behavior to a more active state of behavior. The counselor's task is to encourage the client to reattribute his or her difficulty to a factor or factors over which he or she can control. In this particular case, the client must realize that his or her depressed state is a result of his or her unwillingness to explore other possible relationships rather than because someone has rejected them. This process of reattribution enables the individual to realize that he or she has control over his or her circumstances and can appropriately act upon them. In addition, social influence "theory proposes that therapist's attributional efforts are intended to (1) increase the accuracy of client's attributions so that clients can better guide their own behavior and thus live more effectively and (2) to externalize socially undesirable behavior to diminish and eliminate intense emotional reactions to such behavior" (Strong, 1982, p. 185).

Reattribution Through Interpretation

Social psychological theory has suggested that people are in constant need of attributing their behavior to specific factors. Individuals who do not possess a degree of self-understanding and self-awareness oftentimes attribute their behaviors and emotions to factors which are external to them (Strong, 1982).

Through the process of counseling, the counselor can attempt to generate greater self-awareness and self-understanding in the client. In addition, the counselor can encourage the client to reattribute his or her difficulty to factors over which he or she has control. Recent research on social influence processes in counseling has supported the utilization of the counseling technique of interpretation for encouraging clients to reattribute their circumstances to factors over which they have control.

Historically, the technique of interpretation was founded in psychoanalytic theory. For this reason, many contemporary counselors have avoided utilizing the technique in counseling. Many client-centered-type counselors view "interpretation as the use of a technical vocabulary to impose insights of questionable value on the client, often distancing the client from the counselor emotionally and violating client autonomy" (Claiborn, 1982, p. 439).

Several studies, however, have supported the utilization of interpretation in a social influence context. For example, Strong, Wambach, Lopez, and Cooper (1978) were interested in empirically determining to what degree counselor interpretation contributes to client motivation. Their study included individuals who expressed difficulty dealing with procrastination behavior. The authors felt that the presenting problem of procrastination was useful in this kind of study because procrastination and causes for it can be interpreted in a number of ways. Subjects in the study were randomly assigned to one of three groups. One of these groups was simply a control group, and this group received reflection and questioning as the major counseling techniques. The other two groups received interpretation as the major counseling technique. One group was told that procrastination behavior was the result of deep unresolved conflict with authority figures. Thus, this group's difficulty or static state of behavior was interpreted and attributed to factors which were beyond their control. The remaining group's static state of behavior and their difficulty was attributed to factors which were within their control. The interpretation this group received emphasized that procrastination behavior was simply a result of the individual's lack of planning and effort to accomplish specific tasks.

Treatment conditions were administered by means of one-to-one counseling sessions conducted by one of four trained counselors. After the initial counseling session, each subject was asked to complete a homework assignment which reinforced the interpretation they had received. A second counseling session summarized the initial counseling session and reviewed the homework assignment. In addition, several additional interpretations of procrastination behavior, which supported the initial interpretation, were offered to the clients.

An analysis of the results led the authors to conclude that there was indeed support for their hypothesis. They found that interpretations which emphasized a person's control over factors that contribute to their difficulty motivate clients to change their behavior.

The degree of discrepancy that exists between a counselor's interpretation of a client's experiences and how the client perceives his or her own experiences warrants consideration. This was the position of Claiborn, Ward, and Strong (1981) in a study they conducted on discrepant interpretations. In essence, they believed it was tantamount for social influence researchers to determine what results when a counselor's interpretations clearly suggest that client difficulty is a result of internal factors, while the client attributes his or her difficulty to external factors. These authors hypothesized that large discrepancies between counselor and client perceptions would increase the likelihood of the client embracing the counselor's interpretations.

Again, the presenting problem of procrastination was utilized as had been the case with the Strong et al. (1978) study. The interpretations were similar, in that the external interpretation stressed unresolved conflict with authority figures, while the internal interpretation stressed lack of commitment and motivation on the part of the individual. In addition, these researchers offered varying degrees of the interpretations to the subjects and this proved to be an important factor in the study. In fact, the slightly discrepant interpretation was more facilitative than was the highly discrepant interpretation. The authors concluded that perhaps this was due to the fact that an interpretation which was only slightly discrepant with the individual's attitudes was more understandable and useful to them than was a highly discrepant interpretation.

Two additional studies, one by Hoffman and Teglasi (1982) and the other by Forsyth and Forsyth (1982), have also supported the utilization of counselor interpretation in a social influence framework. In the first study, Hoffman and Teglasi (1982) hypothesized that either an external or an internal interpretation would be perceived as more satisfactory by subjects than no interpretation at all. The results of their study supported this contention and also supported the notion that people do indeed need to attribute their difficulties to some factors, regardless of whether they are internal or external.

Still, Forsyth and Forsyth (1982) hypothesized that interpretations which suggest that clients have control over their circumstances are much more effective than those that do not. In an elaborate, two-part experiment, these authors sought support for their hypothesis by introducing the client variable of locus of control as an additional factor to be considered in the social influence process. Among other findings, the authors noted that the counselor's interpretations were effective as a result of the client's locus of control. Subjects with a high degree of external locus of control benefitted most from the external-oriented interpretation, while subjects with a high degree of internal locus of control benefitted most from an internal-oriented interpretation. Subsequently, those individuals with a high degree of internal locus of control reduced their procrastination behavior.

Counselor Interpretations and Client Dissonance

The counselor who is utilizing a social influence approach to counseling will generate some psychological discomfort in the client as a result of his or her interpretations. This discomfort or dissonance is a result of the counselor challenging the client's attitudes and attributions. Clients come to counseling with certain attitudes and attributions about their difficulties and their behavior, and they are resistant to reformulating these attitudes. However, the counselor's interpretations and attributions generate a discrepancy within the client, and this discrepancy causes the client to realize that inconsistencies exist between himself and his environment. These inconsistencies generate a state of "cognitive dissonance" within the client. Zimbardo (1960) has noted that, "When two or more cognitive elements are psychologically inconsistent (the client's attitudes and the counselor's attitudes), dissonance is created. Dissonance is defined as a psychological tension having drive characteristics. Thus, the existence of dissonance is accompanied by psychological discomfort and when dissonance arises, attempts are made to reduce it" (p. 86).

The client can reduce this sense of psychological discomfort in one of five ways. Optimally, he or she can accept the counselor's suggested reattributions and drop his or her own. Or, he or she can seek out information or opinions that are contrary to the counselor's. Clients can also attempt to discredit the counselor by implying that he or she is unfamiliar with or uninformed about the concerns brought forth by the client. The fourth option a client might choose would be to indicate to the counselor that he or she has decided that the presenting problem is not particularly bothersome and that he or she will probably not pursue the issue further. Finally, the client may try and change the counselor's opinion. Research on social influence theory in counseling has indicated that clients are more likely to accept the counselor's suggestions for reattribution if the client perceives the counselor as someone who is expert, trustworthy, and socially attractive (Dorn, 1984b).

Perceived counselor expertness is attained through several factors. A number of analogue studies have been conducted on perceived counselor expertness and the results support the concept of perceived expertness.

For example, researchers have found that counselors are perceived as experts by clients if they are introduced to clients as competent, knowledgable, and experienced (Atkinson & Carskadden, 1975; Claiborn & Schmidt, 1977; Strong & Schmidt, 1970). Factors such as: a professional-appearing office, professionally appearing attire, and the display of awards, certificates, and diplomas have also been found to contribute to the perceived expertness of the counselor (Barak, Patkin, & Dell, 1982; Guttman & Haase, 1972; Heppner & Pew, 1977; Kerr & Dell, 1976; Siegel & Sell, 1978).

There are several counselor behaviors which have been found to contribute to perceived counselor expertness. These are: the use of direct eye contact (Dell & Schmidt, 1976; Schmidt & Strong, 1970), as well as a direct interview style, occasionally using some psychological terms during the course of the interview (Barak, Patkin, & Dell, 1982), providing interpretations (Claiborn, 1979) and being relaxed and comfortable during the course of the counseling interview (La Crosse, 1975).

The dimension of perceived counselor trustworthiness is achieved through the counselor's open and forthright manner with the client. More important, it is the client's realization that the counselor is involved in the counseling relationship for the client's benefit that generates a solid basis for trusting the counselor.

A few studies have addressed the counselor dimension of trustworthiness in a social influence context. In fact, Rothmeier and Dixon (1980) stressed the importance of the counselor beginning the counseling interview with a discussion of confidentiality. In addition, the use of counselor self-disclosure has been found to be effective in establishing an atmosphere of trust in the counseling relationship, but some question still remains in terms of the differences it generates between male and female clients (Merluzzi, Banikotes, & Missbach, 1978).

The counselor dimension of perceived attractiveness is attained through the client's perception of the counselor as someone who is similar, compatible and socially attractive. The counselor qualities of unconditional positive regard and a non-possessive manner are also aspects of counselor attractiveness.

Substantial research attention has been devoted to the counselor dimension of perceived social attractiveness. Researchers have found that counselor-client similarity (Patton, 1969), physical attractiveness and physical appearance (Cash, Begley, McGown & Wise, 1975; Cash & Kehr, 1978; Lewis & Walsh, 1978; Vargas & Borkowski, 1982), the use of expressive gestures, smiling, and frequent shifts in body posture (Barak et al., 1982; Claiborn, 1979; Strong et al., 1971) and the use of self-disclosures that emphasize that the counselor has had similar feelings, attitudes, and experiences (Lewis & Walsh, 1980, Merluzzi et al., 1978) enhance the client's perception of the counselor as a socially attractive individual.

Measuring Client Perceptions

The *Counselor Rating Form* (CRF) is the most widely used measure for assessing client perceptions of counselors within a social influence framework (Dorn, 1984b). The measure was developed by Barak and La Crosse (1975), and it consists of 36 adjective pairs arranged on a seven-point likert scale. The adjective pairs are opposite in meaning, and after a client visits with a counselor, he or she is asked to complete this measure. Several studies have attested to the reliability and validity of the *Counselor Rating Form* (Barak & Dell, 1977; La Crosse, 1980; La Crosse & Barak, 1976; Zamostny, Corrigan, & Eggert, 1981).

These legitimate concerns, however, have not prevented researchers from developing some creative innovations with the measure. Corrigan and Schmidt (1983) developed an abbreviated form of the measure known as the *Counselor Rating Form — Short Form* (CRF-SF) and Dorn and Jereb (1985) developed and hand-scoring version known as the *Counselor Rating Form — Quick Score* (CRF-QS), and both versions should enhance the usability of the measure for both practitioners and researchers. Perhaps these efforts are a result of the "intuitive appeal" (Heesacker & Heppner, 1983) that the multidimensionality of client perceptions of counselors possesses.

Still, there has been some concern expressed about the measure and the information it provides counseling researchers. For instance, several authors (Atkinson & Wampold, 1982; Corrigan & Schmidt, 1983; Heesacker & Heppner, 1983) have questioned whether the CRF is assessing one counselor dimension, usually referred to as the "good guy" factor (Bergin, 1971), or the three separate dimensions of expertness, trustworthiness, and attractiveness.

In the future, more research attention must be directed toward specific issues related to these three dimensions. For example, the quality of counselor trustworthiness is an important factor in the counseling relationship and yet it has received less research attention than the other two dimensions in the social influence literature (Dorn, 1984b). In contrast, the counselor dimension of counselor attractiveness has received an enormous amount of empirical attention, partly because the factors of physical attractiveness and social attractiveness are oftentimes equated. It is important that those who are interested in the social influence model realize that social attractiveness of the counselor refers to his verbal and nonverbal behavior, while physical attractiveness would be those physical qualities of the counselor (Dorn, 1984B). Finally, in terms of the counselor quality of perceived expertness, some speculation has been voiced about whether counseling as a profession has enthusiastically pursued this counselor variable in part because of its recent preoccupation with professional identity (Dorn, 1984C).

Counselor Social Power

Theoretically, Strong (1968) envisioned that the three counselor dimensions of expertness, trustworthiness, and attractiveness would collectively contribute to the counselor's social power. Strong and Matross (1973) indicated that counselor social power can be traced from the counselor's remarks to the client, the impact these remarks have upon the client, and the response the client eventually exhibits as a result of the counselor's remarks. In short, "if the counselor's remarks imply some kind of change in the client's actions, thoughts or feelings, then the impact on the client will be the stimulation of internal psychological forces impelling the acceptance of change. Forces impelling acceptance can be conceptualized as the counselor's social power on the client" (p. 26).

The following formula was developed by Strong and Matross (1973) in an effort towards conceptualizing the process of social influence:

$$\Delta B = P + (O + R)$$

where:

ΔB = the client's response to the counselor
P = the counselor's social power
O = client's opposition
R = client's resistance

Therefore, when the client complies with the counselor's suggestions, it means that the counselor's social power is greater than the client's opposition and resistance. Client opposition is a result of the client perceiving the counselor's suggestions for attitude and behavior change as being too extensive. Client resistance emerges as a result of the client perceiving the counselor's influence attempts as being incompatible with the counselor's social power base.

Merluzzi, Merluzzi, and Kaul (1977), however, felt that this conceptualization of the social influence process was far too simplistic. Therefore they offered the following formula instead:

$$\Delta B = P(X) + N(Y) = (O+R)$$

ΔB = behavior change

P = counselor's social power base

X = counselor's characteristics

N = client need

Y = client's characteristics

O = client's opposition

R = client's resistance

This formula does the social influence process justice. Without a doubt, the variables of counselor characteristics, client needs, and client characteristics play a vital and dutiful role in the social process. (More on these issues in the next section.)

There are five social power bases from which the counselor working within a social influence framework may operate. Goodyear and Robyak (1981) identified them as: *expert, referent, legitimate, informational,* and *ecological.* These five counselor power bases were described by Dorn (1984b) as *"expert* power emerges as a result of the client's perceptions of the counselor as an expert. Some of the variables that contribute to the counselor's expert power base are during the initial stages of the relationship, the counselor's training, and the counselor's reputation. As the relationship continues to develop, factors such as the counselor's nonverbal behavior, his reflections of the client's verbal material, and his presentation of psychological material will enhance his expert social power base.

Referent power is an aspect of the "perceived attractiveness" of the counselor. This "social attractiveness" emerges from the client's perception that the counselor is similar to him in areas such as personal values, attitudes, and experiences. This social attractiveness gives the client a genuine sense of comfort and assures him that the counselor is personally involved in the relationship.

Legitimate power emerges from the role the counselor holds in society. It is a role that is considered socially acceptable and one that clearly indicates that the counselor is a helper. It is important to realize that clients derive a great sense of comfort and security from the realization that the counselor has no specific interests in the counseling relationship in terms of attaining personal gain. Therefore, the counselor can easily enhance his legitimate social power by stressing these aspects of the relationship and emphasizing the fact that both the counselor and the client are working for the benefit of the client.

Informational power is generated by various sources of information the counselor utilizes in an effort to make the client more aware of his environment and himself. Examples of the kinds of informational sources a counselor could utilize would be books, pamphlets, interest inventories, etc.

The *ecological* power base emerges when the counselor is able to assist the client in controlling his personal environment. Any suggestions that the counselor directs to the client about how he might enhance his own personal environment would be examples of the counselor's ecological power base" (p. 90).

Research on the social power bases of the counselor has been sparse. As of this writing, the following observations have been made through research on counselor social power bases.

During the initial stages of the counseling relationship, most counselors will utilize the referent social power base and gradually ease into the expert power base as the relationship develops (Dell, 1973). When counselors were asked which social power bases they prefer, Robyak (1981) found that counselors use the expert power base with clients of the same sex, but that female counselors prefer to use the legitimate power base with male clients. Along the same line of inquiry, Goodyear, Abadie, and Brunson (1982) examined counselor preferences for certain social power bases as a result of the client's age and the counselor's age. They found that counselors usually utilized the legitimate power base with clients who were of similar age. Finally, Hackman and Claiborn's (1982) study offered a different perspective on the social influence process. Recall that the "perceived social attractiveness" of the counselor was proposed to be a result of the counselor's liking for and similarity to the client. These authors, however, concluded that attitude change is a result of both the discrepancy that exists between counselor and client attitude as well as the degree of similarity that exists between the two individuals.

Client Characteristics that Influence Counselors

Counseling is a process of social interaction that occurs between two individuals — the counselor and the client. Clients seek counseling because they perceive the counselor as someone who possesses the knowledge and the resources to assist them with their personal difficulties and circumstances. However, it is important to realize that even though the client is seeking insight and self-understanding, he or she will also be attempting to either consciously or unconsciously influence the counselor. "The most profound fact of human existence is that the environment people seek to control for their own ends is made up of other people who also seek to control it for their own purposes (Strong, 1982, p. 192). Given this observation, it is understandable why reviewers of the social influence model (Corrigan et al., 1980; Heppner & Dixon, 1981) have encouraged counseling researchers to emphasize the role that client characteristics play in the social influence process.

As is the case with the social power bases of the counselor, research on the role that client characteristics play in the social influence process has been sparse. Merluzzi et al. (1977) considered the client characteristic of locus of control in their study because they believed that it might have a relationship to the client's receptivity to the counselor's influence attempts. Their findings were not significant. This may have been due to methodology, however, because Forsyth and Forsyth (1982) did find locus of control to be an important client variable in the social influence process. Additional client characteristics examined have been counselor-client similarity (Davis et al., 1977), the perceived need for counseling (Heppner & Dixon, 1978), and the ever-present expectations of counseling by the client (Sobel & O'Brien, 1979).

Interestingly enough, it is the author's belief that studies such as the one conducted by Lewis et al. (1981) strike at the core of the concept of client characteristics and the effect that they have upon counselor-client interaction. They considered the variables of client attractiveness, age, and verbal behavior during the counseling session in their study. They concluded from this investigation that while client physical attractiveness may have some minimal initial bearing on the counselor's perceptions of the client, the real issue in terms of client attractiveness is the actual behaviors of the client which facilitate the counseling process, i.e. verbal behavior, self-exploration — those behaviors that do not turn the counseling process into a "rugged struggle" (Dorn, 1984a). The continued exploration of client characteristics and how they contribute to the social influence process should reveal some most intriguing results.

Social Influence Research

Historically, counseling researchers have utilized "analogue studies" in their research efforts. Analogue studies are laboratory studies that simulate the counseling process (Zytowski, 1966). Strong (1971) set forth five guidelines for conducting analogue studies on the social psychological aspects of the counseling process. These guidelines, if adhered to, provide the counseling researcher with an opportunity to generalize his or her findings to the actual process of counseling.

In a review of the research that had been conducted on social influence processes in counseling, Heppner and Dixon (1981) noted that "of the 51 studies that examined events associated with perceived expertness, attractiveness, and trustworthiness, 29 did not meet any of the boundary conditions, 16 met only the first two conditions, five fulfilled three conditions, and only one met four conditions. Over half of the studies reviewed met none of the five boundary conditions" (p. 548). The counseling researcher who is interested in the social psychological aspects of the counseling process should give serious consideration to these guidelines for research. They are as follows:

1. Counseling is a process that occurs between two people—the counselor and the client. The interaction that emerges between these two people results from verbal and nonverbal behavior. The conditions which exist in a laboratory setting should approximate those that exist in a natural setting.

2. A difference in status should be imposed upon the two individuals who are attempting to approximate the counseling relationship. One person is the counselor and the other person is clearly the client. The statements made by the client should be related to his own experiences, and the counselor's remarks should be made in response to the client's experiences.

3. There will be specific lengths of time that counselors and clients will spend together as a result of the presenting problem and the quality of the relationship. The duration of counseling, either short or long term, should be specified.

4. Most individuals who seek counseling have a certain degree of motivation for change. Subjects who participate in laboratory research are not necessarily motivated to change. Therefore, results obtained from subjects in laboratory studies are significant for this reason alone.

5. Clients who seek counseling have a strong personal investment in their behavior. Therefore, researchers using laboratory subjects may

need to identify similar behaviors in these subjects. This will enable researchers the opportunity to greater approximate client resistance in counseling.

Some well-founded criticism has been leveled at the research that has been conducted on social influence processes in counseling, and counseling researchers and practitioners interested in this model must respond to it adequately. Several reviewers have noted the paucity of research that has been conducted on the model in actual counseling settings (Corrigan et al., 1980; Dorn, 1984a; Heppner & Dixon, 1981). A majority of the studies that appear in the literature are "analogue studies," and while they support the internal validity of the social influence model, they offer little to support the external validity of the model.

Gelso (1979) has labelled this continual struggle between internal and external validity the "bubble hypothesis." The difficulties encountered by a counseling researcher are similar to those encountered by a person who places a sticker on a car windshield and finds a bubble underneath it. Smooth it out on one side and it will appear on the other. Answer social influence questions in analogue studies and practitioners will question there validity for actual practice. Discover differences in actual counseling practice and researchers will question their validity due to a lack of experimental control over variables. The solution to this dilemma then would be to examine the variable(s) under question in both analogue and "in the field" studies.

Summary

The social influence model is an intriguing conceptualization of the counseling process. In contrast to the more client-oriented theories of counseling, which focused almost entirely on the contribution that the counselor makes to the counseling relationship, social influence theory places the counseling relationship into the more realistic perspective of examining the process as a two-person interaction in which both parties possess the potential to impact each other.

Of particular interest to practitioners is the umbrella-like quality of social influence theory. It is such that counselors can continue to utilize the more traditional client-oriented theories while continuing to assess their impact through the social influence framework. Rich in historical tradition and contemporary thought, social influence theory as it relates to the counseling process should provide much needed direction for future counseling practice and research.

CHAPTER 2

INTERPERSONAL INFLUENCE THEORY AND THERAPEUTIC INTERACTIONS

STANLEY R. STRONG

INTERPERSONAL INFLUENCE theory is a social psychological theory of the influence processes that underly interpersonal interactions and behavior change through interaction. From the perspective of interpersonal influence theory, counseling and psychotherapy are specialized applications of the behavior principles underlying interpersonal interaction processes, especially the principles governing how behavior change is generated in interpersonal interactions. The purposes of this chapter are to (1) outline the propositions of interpersonal influence theory, (2) present a classification system of interpersonal behaviors and propositions about their functions in interpersonal interactions, and (3) describe therapeutic interactions in terms of therapist and client behaviors, objectives, and changes in the process of therapy.

Interpersonal Influence Theory

Interpersonal Influence theory proposes the following principles underlying interpersonal interaction processes and behavior change:
1. People are proactive causal agents who purposively act on their environments to render the environments hospitable to their survival and development needs.
2. The most important elements of the environments people must render hospitable to their needs are other people. People purposively act on each other to influence each other to behave in ways that bring forth the materials and conditions each needs for survival,

17

growth, and reproduction. Influencing others and being influenced are the most basic of human experiences.

3. Because people must render the behavior of others hospitable to their needs, their behavior is influenced by the behaviors of others.

4. People influence others by how they behave with respect to others. By purposively presenting themselves in specific ways, people manage others' impressions of the nature of the environment the others must influence for their own purposes.

5. Self-presentation and impression management are basic arts of human survival. All aspects of a person's being are engaged in purposive self-presentation to others. Self-awareness and conscious intentions are powerful tools of self-presentation and impression management, but purposive self-presentation is more basic. Purposive self-presentation transcends self-awareness and consciousness.

6. Members of a human community have similar subjective responses to particular self-presentations or interpersonal behaviors. That is, particular interpersonal behaviors generate similar impressions on members of the same human community. Therefore, different interpersonal behaviors can be distinguished and categorized in terms of their impression management (functional) utilities in the interpersonal influence efforts of members of a given human community.

7. Through experience, people learn (1) what behaviors emitted by others are conducive or obstructive to meeting their various needs, and (2) what behaviors they can employ to encourage others to emit various behaviors.

8. Encouraging others to emit behaviors conducive to meeting a specific need of the person becomes the objective of the person's behavior when that need is prepotent.

9. A person's behavior at any moment in an interaction with another is a function of (1) the person's interpretation of the meaning of the other's behavior, (2) the person's objective(s) in the interaction at that moment, and (3) the person's prediction of what behavior on his or her part will encourage the other to conform his or her behavior to the person's objectives.

10. In an interaction, when the other emits a different behavior or the person's prepotent needs change, the person will employ different behaviors in pursuit of influencing the different environment or of conforming the environment to the objectives associated with the now operative need state. This is first-order behavior change. First-

order change denotes the person's contact with dynamic external and/or internal environments.

11. In an interaction, when a person finds that the behavior emitted by another is unexpectedly conducive or obstructive to meeting prepotent needs, the person may change the objectives pursued in service of prepotent needs. When the behaviors the person employs to encourage the other to conform his or her behavior to the person's objectives are unexpectedly effective or ineffective, the person may change the behaviors employed to achieve objectives. These are second-order behavior changes. Second-order change denotes altered understanding of the nature of external and/or internal environments.

12. Whether a person experiences second-order change in an interaction is a function of (1) the experience of unexpected events as defined in 11 above and (2) the importance of the other to the person's need fulfillment (the degree of vulnerability of the person to the other). The more vulnerable the person is to the other, the more likely the person is to experience second-order change when unexpected events occur. The less vulnerable the person is to the other, the more likely the person is to terminate the relationship with the other when unexpected events occur.

Interpersonal Behaviors

Interpersonal behaviors are self-presentations people employ to influence others' behaviors in interactions. The Kaiser Foundation Research Group led by Timothy Leary (1957) concluded, after extensive clinical work with personality measurement, diagnosis, and behavioral observation, that sixteen classes of interpersonal behaviors could be meaningfully distinguished and could be organized in a circumplex model around the dimensions of status and affiliation. Wiggins (1979) intensively studied the psychometric characteristics of interpersonal behavior and personality descriptors and developed a circumplex model of eight classes of interpersonal behaviors that is highly similar to Leary's (1957) model but corrects certain systematic deficencies he found. Working from the Leary and Wiggins models, Strong and Hills (1984) developed a circular model of eight classes of interpersonal behaviors as the framework for a scale for rating behaviors in interpersonal interactions, the *Interpersonal Communication Rating Scale*.

Strong and Hills' (1984) model is presented in Figure 2-1. The eight classes of interpersonal behaviors, arranged in a circular pattern along status and affiliation dimensions, are labeled leading, self-enhancing, critical, distrustful, self-effacing, docile, cooperative, and nurturant. Nurturant, leading, self-enhancing, and critical are dominant behaviors, while distrustful, self-effacing, docile, and cooperative are submissive behaviors. Self-enhancing, critical, distrustful, and self-effacing are hostile behaviors, while leading, nurturant, cooperative, and docile are friendly behaviors. The members of each class of interpersonal behavior are organized along an intensity dimension, with the least intense members falling at the origin of the circle and the most intense on the outer edge. For example, self-enhancing behavior ranges in intensity from self-respecting through self-assured and dominating to arrogant. Self-effacing behavior ranges in intensity from modest through timid and self-doubting to self-punishing.

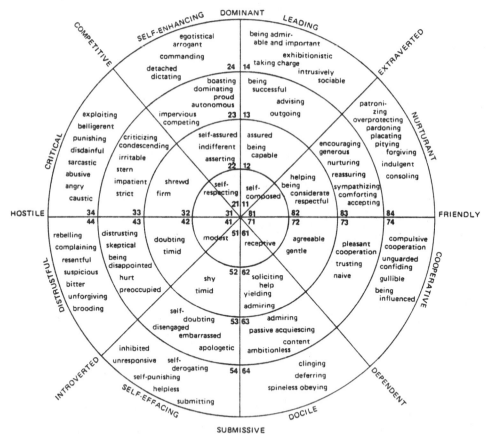

Figure 2-1. Strong and Hills' (1984) interpersonal behavior model.

Each class of interpersonal behavior is hypothesized to convey a particular impression of the characteristics of the actor that invites the other to employ certain behaviors and avoid employing certain other behaviors in pursuit of his or her objectives in the interaction. Each person in an interaction purposively employs interpersonal behaviors to encourage the other to employ the behaviors that fulfill the person's objectives at that moment in the interaction. The interpersonal utilities of interpersonal behaviors are hypothesized to be a function of the following principles:

1. Behaviors at the same level on the affiliation dimension and opposite one another on the status dimension are complements of one another and have opposite interpersonal functions. For example, self-enhancing and self-effacing are complements of one another.

2. Behaviors at the same level on the status dimension and opposite one another on the affiliation dimension are anticomplements of one another and have similar interpersonal functions. For example, leading and self-enhancing are anticomplements of one another.

3. Anticomplementary behaviors encourage interactants to emit the complement of the friendly member of the anticomplementary pair. For example, both members of the anticomplementary pair leading and self-enhancing encourage interactants to emit docile, the complement of leading.

4. Anticomplementary behaviors discourage interactants from emitting the complement of the hostile member of the anticomplementary pair. For example, both members of the anticomplementary pair leading and self-enhancing discourage interactants from emitting self-effacing, the complement of self-enhancing.

5. Interpersonal behaviors exert their strongest discouraging effects on interactant's employment of the same behaviors or their anticomplements. For example, self-enhancing has its strongest discouraging effects on an interactant's employment of self-enhancing or leading behaviors.

6. Hostile members of anticomplementary pairs have stronger encouraging and discouraging effects on an interactant's employment of interpersonal behaviors than do the friendly members of the pairs. For example, self-enhancing has stronger encouraging and discouraging effects than leading.

7. Dominant interpersonal behaviors generally discourage interactant's employment of dominant behaviors, and submissive behaviors generally discourage interactant's employment of submissive behaviors.

In general, the above propositions assert that dominant behaviors invite interactants to pursue their objectives in interactions by employing submissive behaviors, and vice versa. All behaviors invite interactants to employ friendly behaviors, with those nearest the affiliation axis presenting a stronger encouragement for friendliness than for status differentiation. Hostile behaviors are seen as exerting stronger pressures on interactants than their friendly anticomplementary partners. Hostile behaviors incorporate elements of threat embedded in assertions of superiority, lack of interest in the other, criticalness of the other's competence, doubts in the other's fairness or caring for the person, doubts about the other's ability to help the person, and helplessness to deal with issues or contribute to the other's efforts. These elements of threat, not present in friendly behaviors, account for the greater power of the hostile behaviors in interactions.

The elements of threat embedded in hostile behaviors may lead the other to resort to hostile self-presentations of his or her own if his or her objectives in the interaction are strongly held and in opposition to the person's objectives. Redundant exchanges of hostile behaviors in interactions mark determined struggles between interactants to change each other's behaviors using the strongest tools available to them. The behaviors themselves invite the other to employ friendly behaviors that conform to the person's objectives. The other's refusal to do so and determined pursuit of his or her own objectives account for redundant exchanges of hostile behaviors.

Therapeutic Interactions

The purpose of personal counseling and psychotherapy is to generate second-order change in the behavior of clients. From the perspective of interpersonal influence theory, client problems in living are, and stem from, the interpersonal behaviors clients employ in interactions with others. Dysfunctional employment of interpersonal behaviors is a consequence of dysfunctional objectives in interactions or unusual understandings of the relationships between behaviors sent and received in interactions. The therapist's job is to identify the dysfunctional patterns in the client's deployment of interpersonal behaviors, disrupt them, and enable the client to develop more effective deployment of interpersonal behaviors. The therapist must foster the client's degree of vulnerability in the therapeutic relationship so that his or her presentations of unexpected reactions to the client's efforts to conform the therapist to his or her objectives lead to second-order change rather than premature termination of the therapeutic relationship.

A desired outcome of therapy is the alteration of client's objectives in interactions such that their interpersonal behaviors better serve their prepotent needs and are less likely to provoke others to behave in ways that are inhospitable to their needs. Therapists are intensively trained to enable them to purposively use the transforming power of relationships to generate specific changes in the interpersonal functioning of clients, changes that enable clients to be more effective and satisfied members of the human community.

Interpersonal Behaviors and Objectives of Clients and Therapists

Very few studies of the interpersonal behaviors and objectives of clients and therapists have been reported. Raush and his colleagues (Raush, Dittman, & Taylor, 1959; Raush, Farbman, & Llewellyn, 1960) described the interpersonal behavior of six hyperaggressive and acting-out boys in a variety of social situations who were receiving in-patient treatment. Raush and his colleagues compared the boys' behavior to that of six normal boys and to the behavior of the treatment staff in the same settings at the beginning of treatment and one-and-one-half years later. They used Leary's (1957) model for classifying behavior but reported their results in terms of quadrants (hostile dominant, hostile submissive, friendly submissive, and friendly dominant) rather than octents. They found that the boys in treatment exibited much higher levels of hostile dominant and hostile submissive behaviors and much lower levels of friendly dominant and friendly submissive behaviors than did the normal boys, both in interactions with other boys and with the treatment staff. After one-and-one-half years of treatment, they found that the behavior of the boys in treatment had shifted to a pattern more similar to that of the normal boys.

The behaviors of 8 adult clients in 20 psychotherapy interviews drawn from Cutler (1958) and Swensen (1967) are presented in Table 2-1. As points of reference, the behaviors college women employed while working with other women who emitted self-enhancing, critical, docile, or self-effacing behaviors (Strong, Hills & Lanier, 1985; Strong & DeVries, 1985) are also presented. Cutler coded the interpersonal behaviors of 2 therapists and 5 clients in 3 to 4 therapy sessions each, and Swensen coded published excerpts of therapy sessions from Ellis, Rogers, and Wolberg. Both used Leary's (1957) model to code the behaviors. Their results are labeled according to the category equivalents in Strong and Hills's (1984) model to allow comparison among the groups in Table 2-1. Strong, Hills, and Lanier and Strong and DeVries instructed college women to work together in pairs and achieve consensus in creating stories for TAT cards. One of the women was a confederate posing as a subject who enacted self-enhancing or self-effacing roles (Strong, Hills, & Lanier) or critical or docile roles (Strong & DeVries) in the interactions. Both studies used Strong and Hills's *Interpersonal Communication Rating Scale* to code behaviors in the interactions.

TABLE 2-1

PERCENTAGES OF INTERPERSONAL BEHAVIORS EMPLOYED IN
RESPONSE TO THE OTHERS BEHAVIOR IN A CONSENSUS TASK
AND IN PSYCHOTHERAPY

| | others behavior in a consensus task | | | | psychotherapy[3] | |
behavior	self-enhancing[1]	critical[2]	docile[2]	self-effacing[1]	client	therapist
leading	20.3	25.3	58.6	45.8	14.7	34.4
self-enhancing	12.2	5.4	2.7	3.0	7.7	2.1
critical	9.4	15.9	6.0	8.3	.3	17.6
distrustful	4.5	11.3	2.5	1.7	16.5	.3
self-effacing	8.3	9.7	11.2	9.7	32.1	.7
docile	14.2	16.8	2.3	3.6	8.6	9.7
cooperative	23.5	9.4	.4	2.8	19.8	9.8
nurturant	7.7	6.2	16.2	25.0	.3	25.4

[1]Strong, Hills, and Lanier (1985).
[2]Strong and DeVries (1985).
[3]Compilation of Cutler (1958) and Swensen (1967).

As seen in Table 2-1, college women in Strong, Hills, and Lanier's (1985) and Strong and DeVries's (1985) studies responded to dominant behaviors (self-enhancing and critical) by employing a majority of submissive behaviors, and to submissive behaviors (docial and self-effacing) by employing a majority of dominant behaviors. In addition, when the confederates presented dominant behaviors, the women competed for dominance in the interactions by employing self-enhancing when faced with self-enhancing and critical when faced with critical. When the confederates presented submissive behaviors, the women competed for submission by employing self-effacing in response to both docile and self-effacing. Overall, the relatively high deployment of cooperative and distrustful behaviors in response to the two hostile dominant behaviors and nurturant and critical behaviors in response to the anticomplementary submissive pair docile and self-effacing reveals an objective of generating a highly friendly working relationship, an objective stemming from the task instruction to work together to achieve consensus.

Compared to the college women, clients employed high levels of submissive behaviors, especially self-effacing (32.1%) and distrustful (16.5%), and low levels of dominant behaviors, especially leading (14.7%) and nurturant (.3%). The clients were apparently determined to persuade their therapists to adopt a dominant and friendly role in the therapeutic relationship. By employing self-effacing and distrustful behaviors, they portrayed themselves as helpless to assume responsibility and doubtful of the therapists' fairness and trustworthiness, a self-presentation dedicated to propel therapists into nurturant behavior.

Therapists employed high levels of dominant behaviors, especially nurturant (25.4%) and critical (17.6%), and low levels of submissive behaviors, especially distrustful (.3%) and self-effacing (.7%). Compared to college women in dominant roles, therapists employed relatively less leading (34.4% for therapists versus 58.6% and 45.8% for college women) and more nurturant and critical behaviors in their dominance, suggesting a determined effort to persuade clients to employ more friendly submissive behaviors and less hostile submissive behaviors. They also scrupulously avoided distrustful, self-effacing, and self-enhancing behaviors, perhaps to avoid provoking clients to employ even more extreme and persistent distrustful and self-effacing behaviors. Compared to students interacting with a self-effacing other, the therapists employed three times more docile and cooperative behaviors, suggesting that therapists had a second objective of converting clients from hostile submissive interactants into friendly dominant interactants.

The relative proportions of client and therapist behaviors presented in Table 2-1 may have some general descriptive value for psychotherapy. Crowder (1972), using Leary's (1957) model, rated the behaviors of 25 client and therapist pairs in segments from early, middle, and later psychotherapeutic interviews. While he reported his results in terms of quadrants, the proportions he found are very similar to those presented in Table 2-1. Crowder's data suggest some interesting though not large differences between the three time segments of psychotherapy, but he did not analyze the differences.

Contingencies Among Client and Therapist Behaviors

Study of the sequential dependencies among client and therapist in-terpersonal behaviors would reveal the contingencies therapists and clients place on each other in pursuit of their objectives in therapeutic in-teractions. Changes in sequential dependencies during therapy would suggest second-order changes in one or both interactants. Unfortu-nately, sequential dependencies between client and therapist interper-sonal behaviors have not been studied. Mueller (1969) reported the closest approximation to a contingency analysis of interpersonal behav-iors in psychotherapy.

Mueller (1969) coded the interpersonal behaviors of 39 therapist and client pairs in initial and later interviews using Leary's (1957) model. Unfortunately, he did not analyze client and therapist behaviors in terms of sequential behaviors but, rather, intercorrelated the frequencies of total occurrence of eight interpersonal behaviors emitted by clients and therapists over the 39 client-therapist pairs. The correlations may indicate contingencies between client and therapist behaviors, but they may also represent covariation generated by third factors. Some con-tingencies may be masked by the operation of third factors. Finally, whether an observed correlation is due to the therapists' efforts or the clients' cannot be determined.

Changes in the correlations among client and therapist behaviors during the course of psychotherapy can be assessed by comparing Muel-ler's (1969) intercorrelation matrices of therapist and client interpersonal behaviors for initial and later interviews. The later interviews he ana-lyzed were those just preceding significant changes in clients' self-reports on assessment instruments. The relationships Mueller reported are pre-sented in Table 2-2. The labels of behaviors in Table 2-2 have been con-verted into their equivalents in the Strong and Hills (1984) system. Significant positive correlations ($r \geq .30$) are indicated with the symbol (E) and are taken to mean that therapists and/or clients frequently em-ployed one behavior when the other emitted the other behavior. Signifi-cant negative correlations ($r \geq -.30$) are symbolized by (A) and are taken to mean that therapists and/or clients frequently avoided employing one behavior when the other emitted the other behavior. Significant rela-tionships between therapist and client behaviors observed in initial and later interviews are separated by the symbol (/). Significant changes ($\geq .30$) in correlations from initial to later interviews are indicated by ($<$) and ($>$). The symbol ($<$) indicates that the change in correlation was in the positive (+) direction, and the symbol (>) indicates that the change in correlation was in the negative (–) direction.

TABLE 2-2[1]

POSITIVE (E) AND NEGATIVE (A) RELATIONSHIPS[2] AND CHANGES (< >) IN RELATIONSHIPS[3] BETWEEN CLIENT AND THERAPIST IN- TERPERSONAL BEHAVIORS IN INITIAL AND LATER INTERVIEWS[4]

client behavior	lead	enhance	critical	therapist behavior distrust	efface	docile	coop	nurture
leading				A <		<	>	
self- enhance	E /	E / E		E / E				A /
critical		E / E	/ E	E / E	/ E			A / A
distrustful	E >			E >	>			A /
self- effacing		>		>			A /	
docile	A <			A <		E /	< E	E /
cooperative		A / A		/ A				E /
nurturant	/ A	>						/ E

[1]Based on Mueller (1969).
[2]E and A denote positive and negative correlations respectively of $r \geq .30$ ($_{\rho} \leq .05$).
[3]Changes of .30 or more in the degree of correlation between behaviors in initial and later interviews are indicated by (<) and (>). The symbol (<) indicates that the correlation changed in the positive (+) direction, and the symbol (>) indicates that the correlation changed in the negative (−) direction.
[4]Initial and later interviews are noted by initial/later.

Several examples may help the reader grasp the use of symbols in Table 2-2. The correlation between client leading and therapist distrust- ful behaviors was r = – .36 in initial interviews and r = .08 in later in- terviews. In Table 2-2 these relationships are noted as (A<). Note that the "<" indicates change of correlation in the positive direction, not an increase in magnitude. The correlation of client leading behavior with therapist docile behavior was r = −.26 in initial interviews and r = .13 in late interviews. These findings are noted by (<). Since neither corre- lation was statistically significant, neither the (A) nor (E) symbol is used but only the (<) symbol to indicate that the change from initial to later interviews was significant and in a positive direction. Client self-enhancing behavior was positively and significantly correlated with therapist self-enhancing behavior in both initial and later interviews, and is indicated by (E/E).

Interpreting the meaning of the many interrelationships of therapist and client behaviors presented in Table 2-2 will be limited to patterns in initial interviews and changes in the relationships among client and therapist behaviors between initial and later interviews. Because the correlations do not allow determination of who created the observed relationships, they will be looked at twice, once as if clients created the relationships and once as if therapists did.

Assuming that relationships among behaviors in initial interviews were a product of the clients' objectives in the therapeutic interactions, the manner in which clients deployed their interpersonal behaviors suggests that clients had the following objectives.

1. **Discourage therapists from asserting dominance with leading and self-enhancing behaviors.** Employment of self-enhancing and critical and avoidance of docile and cooperative behaviors in response to therapist leading and self-enhancing behaviors reveals an unwillingness to accept therapist dominance through leading and self-enhancing behaviors. Also, avoidance of self-effacing in response to therapist cooperative suggests an attempt to discourage dominance through leading;

2. **Discourage therapists from employing hostile submissive behaviors.** Clients sought to discourage therapists from employing hostile submissive behaviors by employing self-enhancing, critical, and distrustful behaviors in response to therapist distrustful behavior;

3. **Avoid responsibility in the interaction.** The clients avoided assuming responsibility in the interaction both by not emitting leading behavior in response to distrustful behavior and by choosing to counter docile behavior with docile behavior rather than leading behavior;

4. **Encourage therapists to exert dominance with nurturant behavior.** Employment of distrustful against therapist leading and distrustful behaviors, and responding to therapist nurturant with docile and cooperative while avoiding self-enhancing, critical and distrustful, reveals that the clients sought to encourage therapists to exert dominance with nurturant behavior.

Overall, the clients' objectives seemed to have been to **avoid assuming responsibility and leadership and generate a nurturant environment.**

Assuming that relationships among behaviors in initial interviews were a product of the therapists' objectives in the therapeutic interactions, the manner in which therapists deployed their interpersonal behaviors suggests that therapists had the following objectives:

1. **Discourage clients from employing hostile dominant behaviors.** Therapists employed leading, self-enhancing, and distrustful and avoided nurturant behaviors in response to client self-enhancing and critical behaviors, a pattern that would encourage clients to avoid hostile dominant behaviors.

2. **Discourage clients from employing hostile submissive behaviors.** In response to distrustful, therapists employed leading and distrustful and avoided nurturant behaviors. In response to self-effacing, therapists avoided cooperative behavior and most certainly relied heavily on nurturant behavior, but the pervasiveness of their nurturant behavior probably curtailed its correlation with client behaviors. These tactics would discourage client employment of hostile submissive behaviors.

3. **Encourage clients to employ more friendly behaviors.** Perhaps most revealing of this objective was the therapists' employment of nurturant in response to client docile and cooperative behaviors, a response that would create pressure on clients to emit higher levels of cooperative behavior. Therapists avoided distrustful responses to docile and self-enhancing responses to cooperative, probably in an effort to not stimulate further hostile behaviors from the client.

4. **Encourage clients to employ friendly dominant behaviors.** Therapists encouraged leading and avoided discouraging it by employing docile and nurturant and avoiding leading and distrustful behaviors in response to client docile behavior and avoiding distrustful in response to client leading. Employment of distrustful behavior in response to client self-enhancing and critical behaviors invited clients to assume a more caring form of leadership (nurturant) in the interaction. Also of significance is the finding by both Strong, Hills, and Lanier (1985) and Strong and DeVries (1985) in contingency analyses of interpersonal behaviors that nurturant behavior encourages interactants to employ leading behavior, which is more dominating than nurturant but is a friendly and responsible form of leadership.

Overall, the therapists' objectives seem to have been to **discourage client hostile interpersonal behaviors and transform the hostile submissive client into a responsible leader.**

Changes in Client and Therapist Behavior

Changes in the use of interpersonal behaviors by clients and therapists can be assessed in Mueller's (1969) data by examining the client-therapist behavior pairs for which the correlations in initial and later interviews were significantly different. Since Mueller's correlational analysis does not allow determination of who changed, the changes are examined first by assuming that they were due to clients, and second by assuming that they were due to therapists.

Assuming changes in relationships among therapist and client behaviors between initial and later interviews reflected clients' changes in the deployment of their behaviors, it is clear from Table 2-2 that *clients employed distrustful and self-effacing less and docile and leading more* over a broad spectrum. Clients diminished use of self-effacing in response to therapist self-enhancing and distrustful and of distrustful in response to therapist leading, distrustful, and self-effacing. Clients increased their use of leading in response to docile and distrustful, and their use of docile in response to leading. Clearly, therapists had made progress towards their objectives in the therapeutic interaction.

Assuming changes in relationships among therapist and client behaviors between initial and later interviews reflected therapists' changes in the deployment of their behaviors, the pattern of changes in Table 2-2 suggests that *therapists diminished efforts to discourage client employment of distrustful and self-effacing and increased efforts to encourage clients to employ leading and nurturant.* Decreased attention to client distrustful and self-effacing behaviors may have been a function of the clients' decreased use of the behaviors. The emergence of therapist distrustful responses to client leading and docile behaviors reveals therapists' continuing efforts to encourage clients to exert increasingly friendly leadership in the interaction.

The analysis of changes in the relationships between client and therapist interpersonal behaviors reveals that clients changed their behavior to conform to the objectives of therapists. Therapists initially conformed to the nurturant objective of clients, but successfully resisted clients' efforts to propel them into taking full responsibility in the interaction. Instead, therapists manuevered the clients into taking responsibility. Clients apparently were more vulnerable to therapists than therapists were to clients, and the changes in their deployment of behaviors in the therapeutic interactions probably reflected second-order changes in their behavior.

CHAPTER 3

SOCIAL INFLUENCE: TOWARD A GENERAL THEORY OF CHANGE

CHARLES D. CLAIBORN

SOCIAL INFLUENCE has had a positive impact on counseling psychology in two ways. First, it has stimulated a great deal of research on the change process. Second, it has promoted the idea that change is best understood not in terms of particular counseling theories but, rather, change mechanisms that are common to various theoretical approaches. Of course, researchers continue to study (and practitioners continue to use) empathy, frustration, rational restructuring, role-playing, and other interventions derived from a particular theory, but they are less inclined nowadays to view these interventions as explainable only in terms of the theory of origin. They look instead to a more general theory of change, superordinate to theories of counseling, for ways of understanding the counseling process.

Such a theory is more an ideal than a reality. But as an ideal, it serves an organizing and integrative function for much of process research currently conducted. It places that research in the tradition of Frank (1973) and Hobbs (1962), who among others advocated a "common factors" approach to the study of psychotherapy. The social influence model proposed by Strong (1968; Strong & Matross, 1973) extends the common factors approach by showing what a general theory of change would be like and suggesting ways to go about building one. Thus, social influence is not (nor was ever intended to be) simply another counseling theory; it offers no new way of working with clients. Its aim is more purely scientific: to become a theory for considering change independently of the particular theoretical systems within which counseling is conducted. Its aim, in other words, is to be a metatheory, a (scientific) theory about (counseling) theories and their accompanying interventions. As a metatheory, it provides a common language for describing the change process, with concepts drawn from social, interactional, and cognitive psychology. Further, it proposes a basic mechanism of change — influence — in terms of which particular interventions and their effects might be understood.

Social Influence and Interactional Psychology

Interactional psychology is based on the idea that behavior is determined by the interaction of person and situational variables (Endler & Magnusson, 1976). It is distinguished from strictly intrapsychic or behavioral viewpoints, which place the determinants of behavior in either set of variables alone. Social influence may be said to take an interactional view of behavior. To begin with, it shares the four basic tenets of interactional psychology:

1. Behavior is determined by a continuous process of interaction between the individual and the situation he (or she) encounters (feedback).
2. The individual is an intentional, active agent in this interaction process.
3. Cognitive factors are important in this interaction.
4. The psychological meaning of the situation to the individual is an essential determinant of behavior (Endler & Magnusson, 1976, p. 12).

Deriving from these tenets is the notion of reciprocal causality. In interactional psychology, person and situational variables are simultaneously causes and effects. The person acts on the environment as he or she construes the environment, and as he or she expects such actions will affect the environment. Environmental events, in turn, provide the person with feedback regarding the efficacy of those actions and thus shape the constructs, expectancies, and other cognitions that guide subsequent behavior. Social influence retains these interactional ideas but particularizes the concept of environment to refer to the social environment — that is, other people.

Two other interactional ideas applicable to social influence come from communication theory (Watzlawick, Beavin, & Jackson, 1967). The first is the idea that all behavior communicates information. The second is that there are two levels of messages in interpersonal behavior: content and relationship. The content level is literally what is being communicated, most often (if the behavior is verbal) represented in the semantic meaning of the words. The relationship level indicates the kind of message the content message is and, therefore, something about the psychological relationship between sender and receiver. For example, the content message "Act your age!" is accompanied by the (unstated) relationship message "I am in a position to tell you what to do." Relationship messages communicate the sender's attitudes about interpersonal positions that the sender and receiver occupy in the relationship, as well as the sender's expectancies about the range of behavior that the sender and receiver may exhibit. These messages derive from the sender's cognitive construction of the relationship.

Watzlawick, Beavin, and Jackson (1967) called the content level of communication the "report" aspect, because its function is to report information; they called the relationship level of communication the "command" aspect, because its function is to place receiver in a particular position with respect to the sender. The word "command" has nothing to do with the sender's power but emphasizes the idea that the sender's behavior inevitably affects the receiver's behavior. It predisposes the receiver to make certain kinds of responses. To understand communication on the relationship level, one looks not to the behavior itself but to the effects of the behavior on the receiver: In what position does it place the receiver? How does it alter the receiver's range of possible responses?

If behavior in general is determined by the interaction of person and situational variables, then behavior in a social context is jointly under the control of (a) the person's own cognitive construction (interpretation) of events and (b) the behavior of others. It follows from this that the function of interpersonal behavior is to control the other person. "Control" here does not imply coercion as it does in everyday speech. Instead, it refers to having an impact on the other person's behavior—in a word, influence.

This concept of control must be accompanied by three considerations. First, the control is not absolute but probabilistic; each person's behavior makes it more or less likely (but not certain) that the other person will respond in a particular way. Second, the control is not unidirectional but reciprocal; the behavior of each person controls that of the other as they interact. Third, the control is not complete but partial. That is, the sender's behavior is not the only determinant of the receiver's behavior; a second determinant is the receiver's interpretation of that behavior and its social context.

As Strong and Claiborn (1982) have pointed out, an exchange of information on the content level — that is, a conversation — is a negotiation about the relationship on the relationship level. As people interact, reciprocally controlling each other's behavior, they are also sending each other feedback about how well each is doing. Influence takes place on both the content and relationship levels: Influence on the content level results directly from the exchange of information. Influence on the relationship level results from the process of negotiating and maintaining a relationship definition. Moreover, the two levels of influence are interdependent; for example, the success of influence on the content level depends largely on the relationship definition that the interactants have negotiated for themselves. Both levels of influence are important in understanding change in counseling from a social influence perspective.

Two Levels of Influence

Content Level

As Strong (1968) originally proposed it, the social influence view of counseling was concerned solely with change on the content level. Based on attitude change research in social psychology, it focused on how the counselor could establish himself or herself as an influential communicator (in the eyes of the client) and use that position to change client attitudes. The concept of attitude, as used here, refers broadly to the assumptions, constructs, expectancies, and the like that determine the way one sees the world. That world view, in turn, is the immediate determinant of behavior: People respond not to reality itself but to their perception or their cognitive construction of reality. (This is the fourth tenet of interactional psychology, quoted earlier in the chapter.)

Changing client attitudes means changing aspects of the client's world view and, correspondingly, changing particular thoughts, feelings, or behaviors determined by the world view. Attitude change via social influence is the paradigm for change on the content level. The counselor's communications present the client with content that is discrepant from the client's present attitudes. Under the right conditions, the client (according to one process or another, depending on the theory of attitude change) changes his or her attitudes in the direction of those advocated by the counselor. The right conditions for successful influence are the particular combinations of variables known to affect the influence process: characteristics of the counselor affecting his or her ability to influence, the nature and discrepancy of the counselor's communications, and characteristics of the client affecting his or her receptiveness to those communications. Change, as an outcome of counseling, is the collective result of many such attitude changes in the counseling process. Client change—whether manifest in overt behavior, feeling states, or beliefs—is cognitively mediated, because it is both produced and maintained by changes in the client's world view.

The attitude change paradigm contributes usefully to counseling metatheory because, first of all, it is comprehensive in its relevance to different theoretical approaches. Virtually every counseling theory employs concepts of attitude and world view in describing behavior and explaining how its interventions produce change. World view, or its attitudinal components, as the locus of change is a unifying theme in counseling (see Frank, 1973). A metatheory with attitude change as its basic mechanism has excellent potential for transforming this theme into an empirically based principle of change.

A second useful feature of the attitude change paradigm is its parsimonious conceptualization of change: It depicts counseling as an interpretive process. As Claiborn (1982) has argued, any intervention used by the counselor may be considered interpretive if it serves to present the client with a discrepant point of view. Further, the content of interventions, which comes from the counselor's theory, is not important to understanding their effectiveness; interventions from a variety of theoretical approaches can have equivalent effects (see Hobbs, 1962). The important factor seems to be that interventions offer discrepant content at all—that they interpret the client's experience, and, in doing so, influence the client to experience things differently.

All interventions (indeed, all counselor behaviors) may be placed on a continuum representing the extent to which they offer content discrepant from client attitudes. Some behaviors, like nodding and smiling or restating the client's content, offer little discrepancy; other behaviors, from paraphrase and reflection to confrontation, can offer considerably more. Claiborn (1982), drawing upon Levy (1963), distinguished between interventions that offer the client a discrepant language for labeling experience (Levy's semantic interpretations) and interventions that offer the client discrepant ideas (Levy's propositional interpretations). Semantic interpretations, taken collectively, provide the client with a new set of concepts for construing experience (a psychological vocabulary) as well as rules for using the concepts (a psychological grammar). Propositional interpretations more explicitly offer the client new attitudes. Propositional interpretations influence the client to place experiences in a new relationship to one another, or to draw different inferences from those experiences.

The source of influence on the content level is not always the counselor's verbal messages. The counselor's nonverbal behavior can be enormously influential, as well: a smile, a raised eyebrow, a shift in body position all communicate counselor attitudes, especially their more affective and evaluative aspects. Nonverbal behavior is no less powerful as a source of influence because its content is imprecise. It is unfortunate, though understandable, that research on nonverbal behavior has usually examined how it is perceived rather than what messages it communicates. The result is that too little is understood about its interpretive impact.

Still other influential messages do not come directly from the counselor at all, but from the client, in the form of self-perceptions or inner dialogue. The counselor plays an indirect role here by placing the client in situations in which the client will become the source of his or her own influence. One way of doing this is through inducing the client to perform behavior initially alien to his or her repertoire. The increased self-efficacy that accompanies behavior change in, say, participant modeling is an example of how changes in self-perception can result from and actually maintain changes in behavior (Bandura, 1977). Behavior communicates information to the person performing it as it does to others. In the case of self-efficacy, the client's new behavior provides discrepant messages that lead to changes in self-perception. A very different way the client can be made his or her own influence agent is illustrated in the Socratic method (Matross, 1974). Here, the counselor's questions are not directly influential but lead the client to draw conclusions discrepant from prior beliefs. In their own ways, empathic reflections of the client's "incongruence," in the client-centered approach and the Gestalt two-chair dialogue, are variations of the Socratic method. These interventions, like behavior change, make the client aware of discrepancies deriving from his or her own experience, discrepancies that are then dealt with much like those that originate with the counselor. The impact of different sources of discrepancy — counselor verbal and nonverbal behavior, client self-perceptions, client inner dialogue — on the influence process has been little explored.

Relationship Level

Influence on the relationship level contributes to client change in two ways. First, if influence is to occur successfully on the content level, the relationship between counselor and client must be one in which the counselor has adequate social power, or the ability to influence. Counselor and client must therefore negotiate (on the relationship level) relationship definitions that provide the counselor with a suitable base for influencing the client on the content level. Second, the counselor's relationship messages can themselves produce client change. In this sense, influence on the relationship level constitutes a second kind of change, distinct from change resulting from influence on the content level.

Strong and Matross (1973) reconceptualized social influence in terms of interpersonal forces. The force promoting change, counselor social power, results from the relationship definition counselor and client negotiate. In any such relationship, the counselor's social power base specifies the kind and degree of influence the counselor may engage in. Social power characterizes the position of the counselor in the relationship; it is not a quality of the counselor as a person. The client's position as the recipient of influence is the complementary part of the relationship definition and, likewise, not a quality of the client as a person. In fact, counselor and client negotiate the positions they do in order to best control each other in the relationship. The counselor wants the client in a position of optimal receptiveness to the counselor's influence, and will alter his or her own behavior to put and keep the client in that position as long as the relationship lasts. As implied in this conceptualization, the counselor's social power might be expected to change over the course of the relationship, as counselor and client require; such change results from an ongoing relationship negotiation.

Strong and Matross (1973) distinguished two forces working against change: opposition and resistance. The distinction between them directly parallels that between the content and relationship levels of communication. Opposition is the client's disagreement with the *content* of the counselor's influence. Resistance is the client's negative reaction to the *context* of influence — namely, the counseling relationship. The client expresses opposition by generating (covertly or overtly) counterarguments to the counselor's communications. The way the client expresses opposition, of course, is a relationship message; this is why it is so difficult to tell opposition from resistance. But the distinction is an important one, theoretically and practically, because opposition and resistance require very different responses from the counselor.

Resistance is the client's communication to the counselor, on the relationship level, that the relationship between them does not permit the kind of influence the counselor is attempting. In resisting, the client rejects the relationship definition proposed by the counselor and, in the manner of his or her resistance, offers an alternative one. As Freud (1916-1917/1966) recognized (in calling this behavior "resistance neurosis"), the relationship definition offered by the client usually reflects his or her problematic control strategies. Thus, the diagnostic benefit of resistance, as Freud also recognized, is that it brings the client's symptoms into the counseling relationship so that the counselor can see them, feel their effects directly, and counter them. The implications of this are described more fully below.

Client attitude change—that is, change that results from counselor's content messages—requires a relationship that maximizes counselor social power and minimizes the possibility of opposition and resistance. Strong and Matross (1973) state that counselors may be comparably influential from quite different bases, depending on the client's needs and values, the counselor's skill in operating from these bases, and other situational variables. This is the assumption from which most of the research on counselor characteristics—like expertness, trustworthiness, and attractiveness—has been conducted. This research has generally indicated that expertness, and to some extent trustworthiness, are important sources of counselor influence, but that attractiveness is not (see Corrigan et al., 1980). However, the very assumption that different power bases function in the same way may be questioned as Kerr et al. (1983) did in their research on opposition and resistance.

Clearly, continued research on influence in counseling must capture more of its complexity, attending not only to the unique functioning of different social power bases but also to the shifting nature and degree of social power within a relationship over the course of counseling. Conceptualizing social power in terms of relationship definition, rather than stable counselor characteristics, should facilitate such research.

Relationship negotiation not only creates the kind of relationship in which the counselor can influence the client on the content level but also constitutes a second kind of influence on the relationship level itself. Here, the client's symptoms (and the focus of change efforts) are viewed as inadequate interpersonal control strategies. Their defining characteristic is incongruence between content and relationship messages. On the content level, the client expresses a lack of control, like helplessness, confusion, or ignorance. But the accompanying relationship message is controlling; it places the other person in the position of meeting the client's needs. The control strategy is inadequate for two reasons. First, it is indirect; the client places important functions in the hands of others, upon whom he or she must then rely. Ultimately, this makes the client miserable, because the client must develop negative self-perceptions that support the symptom (e.g. "I am depressed"), and these are as stable as the symptom is rigid. Second, the control strategy is deceptive; it appears not to do what it is in fact doing, namely, control. Ultimately, this makes other people miserable, because they are at the mercy of conflicting messages; they know, vaguely, that they do not like the relationship, but they do not know how to extricate themselves.

The counselor has two tasks on the relationship level of influence. The first is to recognize the client's inadequate control strategies and the goals those strategies seem to be seeking. The second is to interact with the client in such a way that those control strategies are stripped of their effectiveness in the relationship with the counselor, and to define a relationship with the client in which "healthier" control strategies will achieve the client's goals. All approaches to counseling have ways of doing this, but nowhere is it a more explicit part of the approach than in the Gestalt therapy of Perls (1969), particularly in the technique of frustration. The Gestalt counselor seeks to understand how the client is manipulating him or her, then responds in such a way as to refuse to let the manipulation work. For instance, if the client acts helpless, the counselor refuses to help — at least in the way the client expects it. If the client acts angry, the counselor refuses to be intimidated, and so on. In responding in a way the client does not expect, the counselor proposes a relationship definition in which the client cannot easily behave in the usual way and must therefore search for alternative strategies to use.

The counselor can observe the client's inadequate control strategies firsthand and actually become the target of them. In a sense, the counselor is both in the relationship with the client and not in it. The counselor interacts with the client, feeling the client's interpersonal impact. Yet, the counselor also observes the client's behavior from a position outside that relationship and makes relatively independent (of the client's behavior) choices about how to respond. Based upon an assessment of the client's inadequate control strategies, the counselor chooses behaviors that prompt the client to adopt alternative strategies in response. Ultimately, the client does adopt alternatives, and if the counselor deems them effective, he or she allows them to have the effect the client wants.

Influence on the relationship level is rather easier to conceptualize than operationalize. Relationship messages are elusive. They must be inferred from content messages, nonverbal behavior, and the context of communication. In addition, schemes for categorizing (and thereby observing) them are few and problematic. Still, a metatheory of change based on social influence must include the relationship level of communication. An integration of this level and the content level into one system, as attempted here and elsewhere (Strong & Claiborn, 1982), might serve to encourage researchers to extend their attentions to this unquestionably important aspect of the influence process.

Summary and Conclusion

Returning to the interactional point of view with which the chapter began, it may be said that change in counseling occurs on both the content and relationship levels of communication, since the client's interaction with the environment and cognitive construction of the environment are interdependent. Influence on the content level most directly affects how the client construes the environment. It provides the client with discrepant information that, through an attitude change process, alters the way the client selectively perceives and draws inferences from events. The counselor may communicate these discrepancies directly in statements to the client or may place the client in situations in which incoming information makes the client aware of discrepancies. Empathic responding, rational-emotive interpretation, and modeling are examples of the direct communication of discrepancy; in each case, the discrepant information originates with the counselor. Behavioral rehearsal, various forms of desensitization, and the Socratic method of questioning are examples of how the counselor may provide opportunities for client awareness of discrepancy; in these cases, the client is (most directly) his or her own influence agent. Influence on the content level, in sum, is characterized by attitude change as the mechanism and the client's world view as the locus of change.

Influence on the relationship level makes influence on the content level possible by establishing the counselor in a socially powerful position with respect to the client. It also constitutes a change mechanism in itself, the locus of which is the client's strategies for interacting with the (social) environment. Here, the counselor provides the client with discrepant — that is, unexpected — consequences for his or her behavior, consequences that come in the form of the counselor's responses to that behavior. The counselor's behavior obstructs the client's efforts to predict and control the environment in the usual ways, and prompts the client to search for alternative control strategies.

Changes resulting from influence on the content level affect how the client construes the counselor's behavior and formulates his or her own response; in doing so, they affect how influence takes place on the relationship level. Conversely, changes resulting from influence on the relationship level—the client's acquisition of alternative control strategies—lead to changes on the content level. They change the way the client construes (predicts) the consequences of his or her behavior on others. And they change the construction (interpretation) of others' behavior as feedback regarding the efficacy of the client's own behavior.

As a promising candidate for a metatheory of change in counseling, social influence has a number of positive features: It is comprehensive, independent of particular theoretical approaches, and strongly rooted in basic psychological research. On the other hand, it has a long way to go before living up to its promise. The bulk of social influence research to date has dealt with perceptions of the counselor along dimensions presumably relevant to social power. As useful as this research is, it concerns only one aspect of the influence process and conveys the misleading notion that this is what social influence is all about. Researchers have paid much less attention to the act of influence—that is, how the counselor changes the client—even though this research tests the premise upon which counselor perception research is based. For instance, how counselors make themselves attractive to clients is important only if attractiveness leads to influence. Researchers have paid still less attention to other aspects of the influence process; the role of the client, in particular, has been completely neglected. But all of this is less a problem with the social influence point of view than simply a direction for future work. Researchers and practitioners alike, in the meantime, must bear in mind how particular research fits in the total picture.

A much bigger problem exists with the influence on the relationship level. Research is far behind theory when it comes to conceptualizing counseling process interactionally. Concepts like relationship definition and control strategy are particularly difficult to operationalize. Further, the notion of reciprocal causality renders many traditional approaches to process research inappropriate. Manipulating interventions or components of interventions in order to assess their differential impact on the client's behavior rather presumes a linear model of change—how the counselor affects the client, rather than how the interaction affects both counselor and client. Pioneering efforts in the linguistic analysis of counseling process and sequential analysis, and the revival of interactional concepts from personality theory, as represented elsewhere in this book, show promise of allowing an examination of the counselor-client interaction as the locus of change. Until these methods are more fully developed and tested, however, it will be difficult for the interactional point of view to gain ground as an empirically based mechanism of change.

CHAPTER 4

EXTRAPOLATING FROM THE ELABORATION LIKELIHOOD MODEL OF ATTITUDE CHANGE TO COUNSELING

MARTIN HEESACKER

RECENT THEORETICAL and empirical advances in social and counseling psychology now allow for major improvement in the conceptualization of counseling as an interpersonal influence process. This chapter expands the application of attitude change theories to counseling by introducing and applying a broadly explanatory, empirically supported and recently developed attitude change theory, the *Elaboration Likelihood Model* (ELM); (Petty and Cacioppo, in press). First, theory and research regarding Strong's (1968) *Interpersonal Influence Theory* will briefly be discussed. Second, problems that have arisen regarding both Strong's theory and data supporting the theory will be highlighted. The third part of this chapter will focus on the ELM. The ELM will be explained and data on the theory will be presented. The ELM's potential for resolving some of the difficulties in applying attitude change theories to counseling will be elaborated and several practical applications of the ELM to counseling research and practice will be made.

In discussing how any theory of persuasion or attitude change might influence the understanding or performance of counseling, assumptions must be made about the place of persuasion in the therapeutic process. Persuasion in counseling can be used to influence several therapeutically important client attitudes: those about seeking treatment; about the counselor's diagnosis; about clients, themselves; about the efficacy of their current feelings, thoughts and behavior; and attitudes about the therapist's treatment plan.

43

Persuasion, like a syringe in medicine, is simply a tool. The topic, extent and direction of therapeutic attitude changes should be determined by the counselor and based upon sound knowledge of the client and of counseling. Persuasion in counseling is not *inherently* beneficial or satisfying to the client, but it can be a powerful tool for understanding and improving counseling. Regardless of the type of therapy, clients must be persuaded (planfully or not) to do the things required in that therapy to be effective (such as freely associating, speaking honestly from the heart, or eradicating irrational thoughts). The broad, practical importance of knowing the best ways to influence the therapeutically relevant attitudes of clients should be appreciated at this level, if at no other.

The Social Influence Model

Theory

This book, along with several others, serves as proof of the important contribution to the field of counseling psychology by Stanley R. Strong's Social (or Interpersonal) Influence Model (Strong, 1968; 1978; 1982; Strong & Claiborn, 1982). As Strong, himself, recently pointed out, "That psychotherapy was a process of social influence was far from evident in the 1960's. Not only was this view not widely accepted, it was widely unacceptable" (Strong, 1982, p. 182). Strong's seminal 1968 paper alerted counseling psychologists, both practitioners and researchers, to the possibility that a variation of Festinger's *Cognitive Dissonance Theory* (Festinger, 1957) could help explain and improve counseling. The publication of Strong's (1968) article broke the stigma long associated with deliberately attempting to influence the attitudes of counseling clients. Most importantly, that article began the practice of integrating social psychological theory with counseling research. As Strong (1978) has suggested, "Psychotherapy can be viewed as a branch of applied social psychology" (p. 101). So, beyond the important direct benefits resulting from the Social Influence Model, Strong's theorizing has facilitated both the acceptance of counseling as an influence process and the appropriateness of using theories from social psychology to understand counseling.

Strong, like several other highly active and creative psychologists, has made refinements and changes in his theory. Most important in Strong's work is the relatively recent shift in emphasis from an exclusive focus on attitudinal change in clients to a focus on both attitudinal and attributional changes (see Strong, 1978, 1982; Strong & Claiborn,

1982). One way of viewing the relationship between the attitudinal and attributional aspects of Strong's theory involves seeing the attitudinal aspect as the process (or "how to change") part, and seeing the attributional aspect as the content (or "what to change") part. Although Strong (e.g. 1978) saw the two aspects as fitting together, they can be seen as discrete. In this chapter, the focus will be on the attitudinal (or original) aspect of the theory.

The initial chapter in this text explains Strong's model. A brief quote from the "Attitude Change" chapter in Strong and Claiborn (1982) will provide the gist of the attitude aspect of Strong's theory and show Strong's emphasis upon the role of cognitive inconsistency in attitude change.

> The attitude change model presented in this chapter considers the underlying mechanism of change to be the creation and resolution of cognitive inconsistencies. Efforts to effect attitude change face . . . [the problem] that there are a variety of responses to cognitive inconsistency, and the individual's choice among them is not always easy to predict . . . . Change occurs to the extent that the source of discrepant information is difficult to derogate and inconsistencies are unavoidable. The importance of attitudes to the individual's functioning, the nature of the discrepancy, and the individual's commitment to particular beliefs all contribute to the unavoidability of inconsistencies and thus to the individual's response to them. [P. 77]

Research

Two critical reviews of the research on social influence in counseling have documented the heuristic value of Strong's theory, with over fifty studies reviewed (Corrigan et al., 1980; Heppner & Dixon, 1981). Readers are referred to these reviews for more details regarding the research. In general, the research has focused almost exclusively on whether clients (or research subjects) perceive different levels of counselor expertness, attractiveness and trustworthiness and whether these different levels result in different amounts of influence over client attitudes. The majority of studies suggest that subjects are able to perceive differences in counselor expertness, attractiveness and trustworthiness. On the question of influence effects, results are more modest and will be detailed next.

Problems Associated with Social Influence Theory

Although in 1968 Strong was wise in selecting Festinger's dissonance theory as the attitude change theory most applicable to counseling, since then, research on social influence in counseling has been quite equivocal in showing attitude and behavior change. Perhaps more importantly, however, recent research in social psychology has seriously undercut several important aspects of dissonance theory. The equivocal data from counseling psychology and the undercutting of dissonance theory from social psychology raise serious questions about the use of Strong's model. The problems arising from counseling and social psychology research will be detailed next.

Counseling Psychology Research

Studies reported in two recent literature reviews have failed to show a consistent relationship between counselor characteristics (expertness, attractiveness, and trustworthiness) and attitude change in clients. Heppner and Dixon (1981) suggested that counselor expertness or attractiveness led to client attitude change in some studies but not in others. Only one study reviewed by Heppner and Dixon suggested that trustworthiness increased the counselor's ability to influence the client (Rothmeier & Dixon, 1980). Similarly, Corrigan et al. (1980) indicated that increases in perceived counselor expertness and attractiveness did not consistently result in corresponding increases in counselor influence.

It should be noted, however, that virtually none of this research assessed the effects of personal involvement, message discrepancy or feelings of dissonance on social influence in counseling. This is despite the fact that Strong had said these factors were important in Social Influence Theory (see Strong, 1968; Strong & Claiborn, 1982). According to Strong's theory, an increase in counselor expertness, attractiveness or trustworthiness should result in increased attitude change, all else being equal. The reasoning for this is that the source cannot be derogated as easily, thus decreasing the probability that dissonance will be reduced through source derogation and increasing the probability that dissonance will be reduced through attitude change. Unfortunately, though, this has not been consistently found. Moreover, no reviewers have suggested, nor have I detected, systematic differences in personal involvement, message discrepancy or feelings of dissonance between studies that did and those that did not support Social Influence Theory.

Social Psychology Research

Research on dissonance theory since Strong (1968) has raised serious questions about the mediational role of cognitive dissonance in attitude change. Hovland's *Learning Model* of attitude change unequivocally associates high source (or counselor) credibility with increased persuasion but without suggesting a mediational role for cognitive dissonance. With the very strong emphasis on source characteristics in counseling social influence research, Hovland's theory is a logical replacement for dissonance theory as the attitude change theory on which counseling social influence theory could be based. Unfortunately, recent research on source credibility effects in persuasion has seriously undercut the applicability of Hovland's theory, as well as the applicability of any other theory predicting a monotonic relationship between source characteristics and persuasion. Social psychology research bearing on Festinger's and Hovland's theories will be discussed next.

FESTINGER'S DISSONANCE THEORY. A primary problem with dissonance theory involves the conditions under which dissonance effects occur. Originally, no requisite conditions were stipulated, but subsequent research has determined that several are, indeed, necessary. First, a person must behave in a manner clearly discrepant from his/her attitude. Second, the person must not have generated thoughts that would rationalize or neutralize the attitude-behavior discrepancy. Third, the person must perceive that he/she had a free choice in doing the behavior. Fourth, the discrepant behavior must be perceived by the person as having negative consequences for self or others (Petty & Cacioppo, 1981, pp. 145-146). It seems unlikely that either counseling or the social influence research to date would consistently possess all four of these conditions, making dissonance theory, and thus Strong's Social Influence Model, less useful in understanding attitude change in counseling.

A second area of research undercutting dissonance theory has questioned whether the person must have a feeling of dissonance in order for the hypothesized effects on persuasion to be found. Bem (e.g. Bem, 1968) has argued that people only need to observe their own behavior (much like another person might) in order to obtain the attitude change that dissonance theory predicts. Bem has shown that the same results that are allegedly caused by internal cognitive dissonance can occur in the absence of dissonance. Fazio, Zanna, and Cooper (1977) provided evidence that, under certain conditions, dissonance theory is operative and, under other conditions, Bem's *Self Perception Theory* is operative. Unfortunately, counseling does not appear to fall exclusively into the domain of either theory. Taking a different approach, Tedeschi, Schlenker and Bonoma (1971) suggested that the attitude changes in dissonance theory research were not caused by dissonance but by subjects wanting to *appear* consistent to other people (like the person doing the experiment). In other words, Tedeschi et al. argued that there was no true attitude change, but rather that subjects pretended to change their attitudes in order to give a favorable impression. Recently, however, Tedeschi has argued that dissonance theory accounts for these effects better than *Impression Management Theory* (e.g., Rosenfeld, Giacalone, & Tedeschi, 1984). Nevertheless, this three-way debate (between dissonance, self perception, and impression management theories) has not been fully resolved and does call into question the essential aspect of dissonance theory (namely, that cognitive dissonance mediates attitude change) and, therefore, the essential aspect of Strong's Social Influence Model (see review by Cialdini, Petty, & Cacioppo, 1981).

HOVLAND'S LEARNING MODEL. Hovland (e.g. Hovland, Janis, & Kelley, 1953) contended that a source (or counselor) of high credibility (an expert and trustworthy person) was more influential than a source of low credibility, because knowing the message was coming from a credible source stimulated the recipient (client) to learn the message better (which resulted in attitude change). Later, Hovland suggested that high credibility led to persuasion because a source of high credibility was associated with good things and that when such a person advocated a certain viewpoint, that viewpoint also became associated with good things and therefore was persuasive. In either version of Hovland's theory, high source (or counselor) credibility should lead to increased persuasion over low source credibility, a prediction central to the social influence research discussed above. Unfortunately for this viewpoint, several recent studies have shown that under certain conditions (conditions that may commonly prevail in counseling), source credibility has *no* effect on attitudes or has the *opposite* effect to that proposed by Hovland.

For example, Sternthal, Dholakia and Leavitt (1978, experiment 2) found that, as Hovland would predict, subjects with prior attitudes against the advocated position were favorably influenced by a source of high credibility. However, when subjects' prior attitudes were somewhat favorable toward the advocated position, the opposite occurred. Subjects' attitudes were favorably influenced by a source of *low* credibility, not high. These data are directly opposite of what both Hovland's theory and dissonance theory would predict. However, they are easily understood using the Elaboration Likelihood Model, to be discussed in the next section. An example showing no source credibility effects in persuasion is provided by Petty, Cacioppo, and Goldman (1981). Petty et al. (1981) varied personal involvement of the subjects, expertness of the speaker, and soundness of the reasoning in the persuasive message.

They found that for subjects low in personal involvement with the issue being discussed, attitude changes were due to source credibility effects but not to message effects. This is consistent with Hovland's theory. However, for subjects high in personal involvement with the issue (probably much like counseling clients), attitude changes were due to message effects and not due to source credibility effects. Again, this pattern of data is easily explained by the ELM but not by Hovland's learning approach or Festinger's Cognitive Dissonance Theory.

The Elaboration Likelihood Model of Attitude Change

Theory

The ELM is a major new approach in persuasion research and has received broad empirical support in explaining persuasion phenomena. The ELM was developed by Richard E. Petty and John T. Cacioppo. It was first published in the 1980's (Petty & Cacioppo, 1981) and only recently has sufficient evidence been amassed to strongly document its potential in understanding interpersonal influence in counseling (see Petty, Cacioppo, & Heesacker, 1984).

The ELM takes into consideration varying degrees of subject recipient interest (or involvement) as a critical variable determining both the nature of attitudes and the extent to which they endure (see Petty & Cacioppo, 1981; Petty & Cacioppo, in press). For example, subjects or clients who are both motivated (personally interested) and able to cognitively process the topic and/or content of a persuasive message are conceptualized as likely to be persuaded by a central route process. Subjects or clients who are not both motivated and able to think about the persuasive message or topic are hypothesized as likely to be persuaded by a peripheral route process. It is important to note that Strong himself (e.g. Strong, 1982; Strong & Claiborn, 1982) has clearly indicated the importance of client involvement in the social influence process.

Central route persuasion involves subjects' own thoughts about the topic and their personal evaluation about the cogency of the arguments presented in the communication. It starts with a persuasive communication, which subjects must be motivated and able to process cognitively. The cognitive response must be predominantly favorable or unfavorable; neutral cognitive responding leads to peripheral route processing. Central route persuasion also requires consolidation into memory of the new cognitions elicited by the persuasive communication. To summarize, central route persuasion is more difficult to obtain but lasts over time and influences behavior more strongly than peripheral route persuasion.

When the conditions for central route persuasion are not present, peripheral route persuasion may occur. In fact, the ELM suggests that peripheral route persuasion can only be effective in the absence of central route conditions. Peripheral route persuasion involves subjects (or clients) perceiving some cue in the persuasion context which is associated favorably or unfavorably with the attitude topic. When the cue is no longer present or recallable, the attitude produced by the cue will not endure, so peripheral route attitudes are said to be elastic. These peripheral route attitude changes are easily produced in the laboratory but do not influence subjects' behavior as strongly as central route attitudes (Petty, Cacioppo, & Heesacker, 1984). According to the ELM, if neither cognitive responding and consolidation nor cue perception occurs, no attitude change should occur.

Empirical Support for the ELM

Although space does not allow exposition of each study, a convincing body of research suggests that, just as the ELM would predict, central route attitudes are based on message content, are mediated by subjects' message-relevant thinking, persist over time, and are predictive of behavior. However, peripheral route attitudes, which are based on contextual cues such as source credibility or likability, are not mediated by subjects' message-relevant thinking, are less persistent over time, and less predictive of behavior, compared to central route attitudes.*

Applications to Counseling Psychology

RESEARCH APPLICATIONS. The ELM holds promise in helping to resolve three *existing* problems in social influence research, namely, inconsistent findings regarding counselor characteristics, little behavior change resulting from client attitude change, and difficulty generalizing from social influence research in the lab to actual counseling. An ELM explanation for the failure of source cues to elicit attitude change consistently involves either (1) that the subject (or client) was processing centrally and thus not influenced by source characteristics or (2) that the person was processing peripherally but that the counselor did not serve as a salient attitude cue.

---

*See reviews by Petty and Cacioppo (in press) and Petty et al. (1984) for detailed discussions of this body of research.

Because many studies have documented that subjects were able to perceive differential expertness, attractiveness and trustworthiness in counselors, the second explanation is not likely. However, the first explanation, namely, that subjects or clients are processing centrally, seems quite plausible in explaining these inconsistent findings. In fact, the inconsistency in findings can be understood using this central route explanation in at least two ways. The first is that these inconsistencies were caused by uncontrolled differences in subjects' thoughts regarding the topic and the cogency of any persuasive message about the topic (and not caused by source characteristic differences). The second involves the knowledge that some people are more likely to engage in central route processing than others (see Cacioppo & Petty 1984; Heesacker, Petty, & Cacioppo, 1983) and by the knowledge that since involvement was not controlled in social influence research, some subjects may have found the topic highly involving while others did not. This subject heterogeneity, which is clearly associated with different attitude responses, may have created sufficient error variance that achieving statistically significant attitude effects became less likely.

A second research problem is that even if subject (or client) attitudes are changed, related behaviors are either not affected or only the very easily performed behaviors are affected (see Heppner and Dixon, 1981). The ELM postulates that strong attitude-behavior relationships are much more likely to occur under central route persuasion, where motivation and ability to cognitively process are high. In addition, this processing must result in clearly favorable or clearly unfavorable topic-relevant thoughts. Since social influence research in counseling has not manipulated variables that lead to an increase in clearly favorable thoughts (such as the cogency of a persuasive message), it is reasonable to conclude that central route persuasion did not occur and therefore behavior change did not occur with attitude change. In the absence of clearly favorable or unfavorable thoughts, a person motivated and able to process must rely on cues for any attitude change. This cue or peripheral route persuasion is much less likely to lead to a strong attitude-behavior relationship.

A third problem commonly associated with social influence research involves external generalizability of laboratory findings to actual counseling (see Goldman, 1978; Strong, 1971). An implication from the ELM regarding generalizability is that the most important dimension on which the lab and field must match, in order for lab results to generalize, is the persuasion route (central versus peripheral). Perhaps not all of Strong's (1971) boundary conditions would be necessary (e.g. #2. status differences), but those associated with higher levels of personal involvement (e.g. #4. motivation to change, and #5. psychological distress and heavy investment in the to-be-changed behaviors) should be very important for generalizability. Perhaps fewer restrictions need to be placed on lab research than had been thought previously. In brief, the ELM can serve as a heuristic regarding external generalizability from the lab to counseling.

Understanding social influence processes using the ELM can result in many important *new* research and counseling applications, as well as in helping to resolve existing problems. The most immediate new applications involve research, but if the theory proves useful in research on social influence in counseling, then applications can responsibly be made to counseling practice. Next, several potential applications to counseling practice will be discussed. All of these should be carefully tested in the lab and via naturally occurring "experiments" before counselors are trained to employ them in counseling.

POTENTIAL COUNSELING APPLICATIONS. If the ELM proves useful in understanding social influence in counseling, counselors may find themselves focusing on the involvement level of clients. This is because attitudes that are most enduring and which have the greatest likelihood of affecting client behavior are those obtained through the central route, and because high personal involvement facilitates central route persuasion by increasing motivation to cognitive processes. Counselors may develop ways to enhance a client's involvement level, to help insure central route processing.

Because the ELM holds that a person must have both the motivation *and ability* to process, counselors may also find themselves making counseling interventions that facilitate the ability of clients to process. For example, counselors may deliberately repeat essential components of their message or may allow clients additional time to simply think about what has been said. Both of these techniques have been shown to increase attitude change (regarding time to think see Tesser, 1978; regarding message repetition see Cacioppo & Petty, 1979). An ELM theorist would contend this is because these techniques increase the ability to process the topic and/or content of the message.

Perhaps the most striking applications that could be made to counseling, if the theory proves useful in understanding counseling, involve a focus on the persuasive characteristics of the counselor's comments in counseling. The ELM holds that under central route processing, the client's thoughts determine his or her attitude. These thoughts about the topic can be influenced by the content of the persuasive communication that the client hears (in this case, the counselor's remarks). If the client finds the content of these remarks compelling, attitude change should result. Counselors, then, could be trained to employ the kind of arguments that clients find most compelling as a way of influencing client attitudes and behavior.

Conclusions

This chapter has briefly highlighted the contributions of Strong's (1968) Social Influence Model and has discussed some of the more recent research that suggests the need for some refinements in the original model. The Elaboration Likelihood Model of attitude change was introduced as a way to facilitate this refinement process. Importantly, the ELM is responsive to Strong's own concern about client involvement level as an important factor in the influence process (e.g. Strong, 1982). Finally, research supporting the ELM was discussed and several practical applications to counseling psychology were made.

CHAPTER 5

ELABORATION LIKELIHOOD AND THE
COUNSELING PROCESS*

CAL D. STOLTENBERG

THIS CHAPTER will build upon the concise presentation of the ELM by Martin Heesacker in the preceding chapter, paying particular attention to the potential applications of this model for counseling practice and research.

The Routes to Persuasion

The ELM views the individual as an active processor of information, and the focus of persuasion, then, is to examine how this process can be influenced by source, message, and recipient factors in the persuasion setting. Petty and Cacioppo (1981) have noted that this processing of information can be represented by a continuum with two quite different routes to persuasion at the extreme poles. One of these, called the *central route,* views attitude change as resulting from a careful and intensive consideration of information pertinent to the issue at hand. Although change via the central route is difficult to achieve, this cognitive processing is probably most similar to what counseling and psychotherapy are designed to achieve. The most facilitative form of central route processing would consist of weighing carefully the pros and cons of a particular action or position, listening carefully to and evaluating what the counselor has to say, searching one's memory for other important informa-

---

*The author would like to thank John T. Cacioppo, Richard E. Petty, and John H. Harvey for their helpful comments on an earlier draft of this chapter.

tion, and deriving a reasoned position or plan of action. Another form, perhaps more common in counseling, consists of biased processing by the client resulting in an attack on arguments presented by the counselor.

At the other end of the continuum we have the *peripheral route* to persuasion which is characterized by less of an inclination by the individual to expend cognitive effort to derive an attitude. Unfortunately, this approach to information processing may also be typical of clients. Peripheral route processing consists largely of looking for cues in the persuasion situation to derive a simple decision rule in forming an attitude. Relevant cues might include the attractiveness or likability of the source, the perceived credibility of the source, or the number of supporting arguments (cf. Cacioppo, Petty, & Stoltenberg, 1985). In the counseling situation, this might take the form of agreeing with the counselor's interpretation of an event because he or she is viewed by the client as being an expert and, thus, must have developed a reasoned position. Utilizing this route to attitude formation saves the client considerable effort as it becomes unnecessary to diligently evaluate information relevant to the issue at hand. Thus, the client's attitudes may temporarily shift without a significant change or addition to his or her conceptual store of arguments in support of the attitudes.

As the reader is already aware, these two routes to persuasion have different behavioral consequences. Evidence is accumulating that indicates attitudes derived from processing information via the central route persist longer and are more predictive of subsequent behavior than attitudes resulting from peripheral route processing (Cialdini, Petty, & Cacioppo, 1981). This conceptualization of the attitude-behavior link fits well with research from the counseling literature. Investigations of the interpersonal influence model of counseling have been largely supportive of the ability of the counselor (or analogue counselor) to elicit temporary attitude change on the part of the client (Corrigan et al. 1980; Heppner & Dixon, 1981). However, some difficulty has been noted in translating this attitude change to behavioral change in the client (Stoltenberg & McNeill, 1984). As we will see later in this chapter, such difficulties in behavioral compliance may be traced to a reliance on attitude change via the peripheral route in these studies resulting in less commitment on the part of the client to change.

Motivation and Ability

A common perception among counselors and therapists is that motivated clients are more likely to continue in the counseling relationship and show improvement than non-motivated clients. The motivated client will tend to diligently consider pertinent information (central route), while the unmotivated client will be more likely to search for peripheral cues to guide his or her decision making or retain previously held attitudes.

How does a counselor increase a client's motivation? In laboratory research on the ELM, motivation has primarily been manipulated by altering the perceived personal relevance of an issue for the subject (Petty & Cacioppo, 1981). Our own counseling analogue research has found that an individual's degree of decisiveness on an issue can affect his or her "elaboration likelihood" or motivation to process a message. For example, we have found subjects who show a high degree of career decisiveness report listening to a career counseling interview as less personally relevant (less important) than subjects indicating a low degree of career decisiveness (Stoltenberg & McNeill, 1984). This difference in perceived personal relevance of the issue had differential effects on message processing, as highly involved subjects rated the counseling session and the counselor more positively than less involved subjects. This effect appeared to be due to greater attention to the high-quality "message" by the involved than the uninvolved subjects. Thus, we may assume that clients will be more likely to engage in central route processing if they view the issues addressed in counseling as important or personally relevant to them. One might increase this perceived personal relevance by highlighting to the client the consequences of continuing current dysfunctional behaviors compared to the projected consequences of alternative behaviors. As Garfield (1980) notes, the theoretical rationale presented by the therapist is of great importance in inducing change in the client. For this to occur, however, the individual must be ready to consider carefully the therapist's conceptualization of the problem.

Investigations of the interpersonal influence process in counseling have typically not addressed the effects of issue involvement on persuasion. Attempts have been made to assess the effects of issue involvement by examining levels of subject or client "perceived need" or request for help (Heppner & Dixon, 1978; Dixon & Claiborn, 1981), and motivation for counseling (Heppner & Heesacker, 1982) with no differential effects noted. However, perceived need or motivation for counseling may not be precisely tapping the personal relevance of issues specific to problem resolution. For example, we might find clients who are "committed" to coming in for weekly counseling sessions but are not sufficiently committed to evaluating and engaging in changing their behavior. Dixon and Claiborn (1981) have probably come the closest to this conceptualization of issue involvement by defining client need in terms of "commitment to change." In their study, subjects who were induced to list reasons why it is important to think about and make a career decision, and commit to relevant out-of-session behaviors by signing a written contract, demonstrated higher compliance with the homework assignments than subjects in the low-commitment condition. The initial manipulation, listing reasons for performing the task, was not designed to elicit a desire in the subjects to form a veridical position on the issue; a necessary condition for central route processing. However, it is possible that it had, at least partly, this effect. No differences were reported for the attitude change measures, however, suggesting that peripheral route processing may also have been active in affecting attitudes in the low commitment group.

Procedures have been described in the literature for increasing client motivation to change. For example, Rogers (1984) has used fear appeals to increase subjects' motivation to give up cigarette smoking. This approach highlights the negative consequences of a current behavior to increase the person's motivation to consider ways to change and adopt alternative behaviors. Garfield (1980) has noted the importance of the therapist's confidence in his or her approach to therapy as an influential factor in client improvement. Quite likely, this conveyed confidence serves to motivate the client to consider the conceptualizations and suggestions offered by the therapist, therefore increasing the likelihood of central route processing.

Thus far, we have focused on the positive aspects of client motivation to process information in counseling. The most obvious negative result of low motivation is premature termination of therapy. An equally troublesome, though less obvious, consequence of low elaboration likelihood is temporary attitude change in the client that decays over time and doesn't result in behavior change. Recall that peripheral route processing (attending to persuasion cues in the counseling setting) can also result in attitude change. Such attitudes, however, tend to be transient and do not lead to altered behaviors (Cialdini et al., 1981). Thus, one might note agreement by the client with the counselor's interpretations and treatment plan only to discover at a later date that such agreement did not persist and little (if any) compliance with homework assignments ensued. In other words, the client may assume that you know what you are doing and agree with your treatment plan (after all, you are the counselor) but will lack the motivation to diligently consider the costs and benefits of such a program and, consequently, will not invest much energy in the counseling process. Such clients often become "no-shows" and counseling can end in premature termination. In contrast to this position, however, it has been suggested by Cacioppo et al. (1985) that the peripheral route may be useful in inducing a client to try out certain low-cost behaviors. Initial success may then provide adequate motivation for subsequent behavior change.

Practicing counselors and therapists are familiar with the problems associated with counseling clients who perceive the process as unimportant or lacking value for them. Such perceptions are common among clients referred to counseling. It is not uncommon for these referred (and sometimes even self-referred) clients to come to therapy apparently prepared to resist or argue with the therapist's interpretations and suggestions for change. In such cases, it appears that the client has come to counseling with a negative bias with which he or she will process information provided by the counselor. This is similar to the process reported in social psychological laboratory studies investigating the effects of *persuasive-intent* forewarnings for personally relevant appeals (Petty & Cacioppo, 1979). Another form of "resistance" results from the client's foreknowledge of the issues to be addressed in counseling and anticipation of the therapist's likely position on those issues. The personal relevance of these issues can cause the client to rehearse supporting arguments for his or her attitudes and behaviors in a manner similar to laboratory studies investigating *topic and position* forewarnings (e.g. Cacioppo & Petty, 1979). As Cacioppo et al. (1985) have noted, this client resistance should be dealt with to allow for subsequent change. For clients exhibiting a negative bias in therapy (persuasive-intent), emphasizing the goal of collaboratively evaluating alternatives with the client making the final decision may reduce resistance. In the second situation (topic and position), this information may prove useful in understanding the breadth and depth of the client's thinking on the issue and serve to identify alternatives that have already been tried or evaluated.

Aside from these circumstances, however, one might assume that most clients do see the personal relevance of counseling and the issues dealt with during their sessions. I would like to suggest, as Petty and Cacioppo (1979) have previously noted, that personal relevance or issue involvement may in fact interact in a curvilinear fashion with the client's elaboration likelihood. Thus, when a client finds an issue too important (perhaps, too threatening), we may find a tendency for him or her to engage in peripheral route processing or, in extreme cases, avoidance of information processing.

An implicit assumption associated with many orientations to psychotherapy is that cognitive, emotional, and behavioral aspects of an individual's functioning must be examined in order for lasting improvement to occur. According to this position, focusing solely on the client's cognitions and behavior will result in, at best, temporary improvement and the problems can be expected to surface again in the future. Such clients may present themselves in therapy in at least two ways. At one extreme we will see a client who intellectualizes his or her problems and comes to the counselor seeking rational prescriptions for improvement. It may also be possible for an individual to resist diligent processing of information while displaying extreme emotional turmoil. The client who reacts to personal crises by dropping into a severe case of depression will also be unlikely to adequately assess his or her situation and generate and evaluate alternatives. Again, we might conceptualize this as over-involvement or extreme personal relevance (as perceived by the client) resulting in a reluctance (or inability) to engage in an effortful examination of the problem, but rather exhibiting a negative set towards new information. In certain circumstances, however, clients will agree with the counselor's conceptualization of the problem and recommendations for dealing with it but later lack the behavioral commitment to assist in generating and complying with the treatment plan. Thus, as illustrated in both of the above examples, the degree and appropriateness of a client's emotional reactions to life events may serve as a cue to the counselor of the likelihood of either central or peripheral processing of pertinent information.

The characteristics of the recipient or client will interact with the message to influence the type and degree of information processing that occurs. Social psychological research has identified "need for cognition" and field dependence/independence (cf. Cacioppo et al., 1985) as recipient factors that influence the person's propensity for either central or peripheral route processing. Our own research indicates that the cognitive style of an individual may affect his or her perceptions of the viability of various counseling approaches as well as the person's attitudes toward the counselor. Using a "thinking" and "feeling" measure of cognitive style, we found thinking-type subjects rated the quality of a counseling session using a rational-emotive therapy approach higher, rated the therapist as more credible, and reported that they were more likely to consider seeking out such a therapist in the future than the feeling types (Stoltenberg, Maddux, & Pace, 1986).

The client's ability to process information must also be considered in eliciting enduring attitude change and related behaviors. A client who is unable to understand or comprehend the message given by his or her therapist will be unable to diligently process that message and enduring attitude change will be difficult. Research in counseling suggests this limitation on message processing exists for the use of therapeutic jargon and when a lack of sufficient familiarity with the counseling process or issues addressed in counseling exists (cf. Cacioppo et al., 1985). Using appropriate language and informing the client about the therapy process can be viewed as providing a central route or "set" for the client which highlights the importance of cognitive effort on the part of the client for therapy to be successful.

The Nature of Cognitive Processing

There is evidence to suggest that subjects are less likely to engage in central route processing when the recommendation from a source is pro-attitudinal (one with which the recipient is already in agreement), particularly if it relates to an issue for which the subject lacks personal involvement (Cacioppo & Petty, 1979). In essence, the subject appears to perceive little need for a careful consideration of the message when he or she already agrees with the recommendation and the source is perceived as an expert. Thus, the persuasive advantage may actually shift to a source of less credibility if the message presents cogent arguments and the issue is not viewed as personally relevant. Conversely, when the source is perceived to be of moderate or uncertain credibility, and other peripheral cues are absent in the persuasion setting, the subject is more inclined to attend to the message to derive a position. Thus, if the message presents cogent arguments in support of the recommendation, more persuasion can result in response to the moderately credible source than the highly credible source due to more attention paid to the message.

Consider, for example, a client who comes to a university counseling service for help with career decision making. She already believes that deciding on a career will help her choose a major and direct her studies in school, and she hears recommendations to that effect from her counselor (who is likely to be viewed as a credible source). A series of activities are planned to help her explore her interests, abilities, and career options, but the client finds it difficult to follow through with this plan due to the many forms of interference or distraction present in her environment (e.g. parties, talking with friends, etc.). Unless this client becomes convinced of the personal relevance of this issue, she is unlikely to consider in any depth the pros and cons of the treatment plan and her commitment to it is likely to waiver. The first order of business for the counselor, then, is to make the personal relevance of this issue salient to the client in order to encourage an effortful consideration of the advantages and disadvantages of the various options.

Counselor Credibility

Research on Strong's (1968) interpersonal influence model has used various operationalizations of factors associated with counselor verbal and nonverbal behavior. In terms of the ELM, we might consider these behaviors to be peripheral cues in the persuasion setting, or similar to specious arguments affecting message quality (cf. Cacioppo et al., 1985). Thus, evidential or reputational cues would be considered source or counselor expertness manipulations, while the behavior of the counselor would be an aspect of the message provided.

Approaching the literature from this perspective may add some clarity to the results of many of these studies. For example, reputational or other evidential cues have yielded mixed and inconclusive results on subject attitudes. In addition, some studies have found that expert counselors produce more attitude and behavior change than non-experts, while others have reported expert and non-expert counselors produce about the same amount of change (see Corrigan et al., 1980, and Heppner & Dixon, 1981, for reviews). If we redefine counselor behaviors as part of the message, they can then be viewed as either confirming or disconfirming the reputational or evidential expertness manipulations. It would not be surprising, then, that these manipulations of counselor behaviors (as message quality manipulations) would also affect ratings of counselor expertise. Indeed, Stoltenberg and McNeill (1984) noted effects consistent with this position. According to the ELM, these source or counselor characteristics will either serve as peripheral cues or serve to elicit increased central route processing by the client. Approaching research on counseling in this manner may prove useful in more accurately predicting the outcomes of persuasive communications by the counselor on client attitudes and behavior.

In social psychological and counseling laboratory studies, message quality is consistently found to produce the most pronounced effects on attitudes and behaviors (especially under conditions of high issue involvement) in comparison with manipulations of source or counselor credibility (e.g. Stoltenberg & Davis, 1985). However, this effect for message quality is typically mediated by source credibility and issue involvement manipulations. Petty and Cacioppo (1981) have noted a greater likelihood of subjects to attend more closely to counterattitudinal messages from a source of high rather than low credibility when the issue is personally relevant. The notion is that the subjects see the relevance of the issue and expect to hear veridical information from an expert source, thus allowing them to derive an educated position on the issue. In this situation, source (or counselor) expertness would serve as a cue to the subject to engage in central route processing. When the issue lacks personal relevance for the subject, however, the expertness of the source serves as a peripheral cue and reduces the likelihood that the message will be attended to and elaborated upon. The reader will also recall that proattitudinal recommendations have been found to demonstrate more clearly this added effect of source expertness on message processing under conditions of high involvement. Under low involvement conditions, however, less credible sources appear to have an edge in eliciting or cuing central processing (Stoltenberg & Davis, 1985).

Let us return to how this can affect the counseling process. Counseling can be viewed as a sequence of discussions on topics concerning the client. Some of these topics are likely to be viewed as personally involving by the client, while others will be perceived as not particularly relevant (although these will likely be viewed by the counselor as relevant). For those involving issues, the perceived expertness of the counselor can be viewed as a definite plus in eliciting central route processing on the part of the client. For issues the client fails to see as particularly relevant, however, viewing the counselor or therapist as an expert may actually reduce the processing of relevant information and inhibit the development of positive attitudes and subsequent behavior change. In reviewing relevant counseling studies, it is difficult to identify the level of issue involvement likely for subjects participating in investigations of the effects of counselor expertness on attitudes and behavior. It is equally difficult (in most cases) to ascertain if the messages contained in these studies were pro-or counterattitudinal for the subjects, or whether they were high-or low-quality messages. Thus, sorting out the relative effects of these factors is difficult and may contribute to the inconsistent findings noted in reviews of the literature (e.g., Corrigan et al., 1980; Heppner & Dixon, 1981). Attending carefully to source (counselor characteristics), message (counselor verbal and nonverbal behavior), and recipient (client characteristics and level of involvement) factors in future counseling and analogue research should prove helpful in assessing their relative effects on attitudes and behavior.

Conclusion

The ELM presents us with a complex coherent or integrative picture of the interactions among variables related to the factors of source, message, and recipient characteristics in persuasion. It has been noted how source or counselor expertness can either enhance or inhibit central or peripheral route processing depending on recipient factors (e.g. motivation and ability, need for cognition, etc.). It has also been noted that attitude change can result from either route, although we have suggested that central route processing is probably the preferred route in counseling. Finally, the content of the message itself becomes important in central route processing, as the client or subject will be critically evaluating what the source or counselor is suggesting.

Due to the fairly recent conceptual application of the ELM to counseling and psychotherapy, little direct empirical evidence exists in support of the viability of the ELM for this persuasion context. Still, the parallels noted between social psychological laboratory research and counseling research and practice are encouraging in suggesting the potential value of this model for counselors and psychotherapists.

Because of its comprehensive view of persuasion, the ELM offers considerable explanatory (and, perhaps, predictive) power for the counseling process and outcome researcher. By keeping the interactive effects of the posited influential factors in mind, the counseling practitioner may also find the model useful in designing and implementing interventions with clients. As is probably evident by this point, the ELM should not be considered a theory of counseling or psychotherapy but a model by which other theories can be evaluated and, perhaps, revised. As Garfield (1980) notes, the process of persuasion is common to all forms of psychotherapy. Thus, the most valuable contribution of the ELM in the future may be in its usefulness in further specifying the persuasion process as it occurs within existing therapeutic orientations.

CHAPTER 6

UNDERSTANDING CLIENT VARIABLES
IN THE SOCIAL INFLUENCE
PROCESS

BARBARA A. KERR, DOUGLAS H. OLSON,
TERRY M. PACE, AND CHARLES D. CLAIBORN

THE EXCITEMENT generated by Strong's interpersonal influence model of counseling (1968) led to great quantities of research focusing on the counselor characteristics of expertness, attractiveness, and trustworthiness. Much of this research has been helpful to counselors and counselor educators. By simply learning particular cues and strategies related to client perceptions of expertness, attractiveness and trustworthiness, counselors were able to increase the effectiveness of their influence attempts. Kerr, Claiborn, and Dixon (1982) summarized three sets of "persuasion skills" that could be taught to counselors in training. Strong's original model, however, made mention of another important set of variables — client variables — which were not seized upon as avidly by researchers. Client variables are a great deal more difficult to study than counselor variables. After all, counselors (usually one's colleagues) don't object to having aspects of their attire, demeanor, and verbal behavior altered in order to test the impact of these variables on the client. Clients, however, are not as manipulable, and finding species of clients other than the non-resistent college sophomore with academic or career concerns is as difficult as finding alternatives to the white rat for the psychological laboratory.

Nevertheless, client variables *are* important to an understanding of the social influence model of counseling, and appropriate assessment of client variables is likely to be crucial to the successful outcome of counseling. The question must be, "Which client characteristics predispose clients to be influenced or affect persuasibility?"

Three areas of research have something to tell us about which client characteristics are related to persuasibility. These are social psychological research on "receiver characteristics," information processing research on response to influence, and clinical/counseling research relating client variable to counseling outcome.

Social Psychological Research

Social psychologists studying the influence process have long been interested in the characteristics of receivers of influence attempts that make them more likely to be persuaded. There are both stable factors such as demographic variables and situational factors such as expectations or mood to be considered (McGuire, 1969). Gender is one of the most important stable variables: females seem to be more persuasible than males. Age is another important variable: people seem to become persuasible as they get older. Perhaps, as Eagly (1983) suggests, both of these facts are related to status differences. Women have less status than men in our society, and most are brought up internalizing this lower status. As people get older, they generally increase in status, at least until they are very elderly. Therefore, women may be more likely to be receptive to influence than men, and younger people may be more receptive to influence than older people.

Some personality traits seem to be related to persuasibility, but the relationships are always complex. People with high self-esteem may be less persuasible than people with low self-esteem (Eagly, 1967).

Cognitive abilities also seem to play an important role in an individual's receptivity to influence. It may be that average or higher-than-average cognitive skills of the receiver are as important to the success of the influence process as those of the communicator. After all, influence usually consists of verbal arguments. The ability of the receiver to understand the communicator's vocabulary and concepts, as well as the receiver's ability to follow an argument, are probably crucial to the outcome of the influence process. Therefore, intelligence, cognitive style, and decision-making ability (MacGuire, 1969) have all been investigated in terms of their relationship to persuasibility.

Some receiver characteristics that are important in determining influencability are tied to the particular situation. Ego involvement, that is, the condition in which the receiver considers the information in the influence attempt to be very personally relevant to him or her, is probably strongly related to whether the receiver is influenced. However, ego involvement is likely to interact with perceived discrepancy of the message (Rhine & Severance, 1970). In other words, if a receiver is very ego involved and the message is very discrepant (disagrees with the receiver's attitude), then change is less likely. On the other hand, if the ego-involved individual receives a message which is only moderately discrepant, change may be more likely (Strong & Claiborn, 1982).

Two other receiver variables are concerned with what the receiver does in the influence situation: active participation and behavioral commitment. Social psychological research has shown that when the receiver plays an active role in the influence process, more attitude change occurs (Weick, 1964). For instance, if a person actually has to develop a speech or role-play involving the desired new attitude, he/she is more likely to change. Behavioral commitment leads to attitude change when, during the influence process, the receiver publicly expresses a position. So, if an individual, in the presence of others, commits himself or herself to a discrepant attitude, then change is more likely (Cohen & Latane, 1962).

Finally, the actual mood or level of arousal of the receiver may be related to persuasibility. Some research has shown that when people receive messages that disagree with their beliefs, physiological arousal is increased (Croyle & Cooper, 1983). In addition, mood states can create altered arousal. How arousal is related to attitude change is not yet understood, but certainly it will continue to fascinate social psychological researchers.

Information Processing Research

Social psychologists have often pointed out that characteristics of the sender and receiver of persuasion cannot, by themselves, account for the success or failure of an influence attempt. How the receiver processes, or thinks about, the influence message is also of great importance. Only recently, however, have techniques such as the cognitive response analysis been perfected which allow psychologists to analyze the thinking processes of a person who have just been the recipient of an influence attempt.

Cognitive response analysis is concerned with how individuals elaborate upon information (Cacioppo & Petty, 1981). The most important variables to the research are the direction (favorable vs. unfavorable) and the amount of issue relevant cognitive responding. All kinds of cognitive responses need to be considered: recognitions, associations, elaborations, ideas, and images (Cacioppo, Harkins, & Petty, 1981). The technique most commonly used to measure the direction and amount of cognitive responses is the thought-listing technique (Cacioppo & Petty, 1981). This technique involves asking an individual during the persuasion process to list all thoughts, images, associations, etc. which occur to him/her.

The hypothesis of this research which holds the most interest for the counselor is the Elaboration Likelihood Model (ELM) of attitude change (Petty & Cacioppo, 1981). According to this model, there are two routes that receivers may take to attitude change: the central or the peripheral route. If the individual who has just received an influence attempt starts thinking about and elaborating on the argument that has just been made, then the central route has been taken.

If, instead, the individual neglects to think about the argument but rather makes some decision about the issue based on superficial cues — such as the attractiveness or the apparent expertness of the persuader — then the peripheral route has been taken. Now, the central route has been found to lead to more enduring attitude change (Chaiken, 1980), so it is certainly the route that the persuader hopes that the receiver will choose. If the receiver will think about and elaborate upon the argument, the change will be more lasting than if he/she forms a quick judgment based on contextual cues. In fact, the persuasion proceeding by the peripheral route may only remain as long as the contextual cues are in place. Many people have noticed how particularly charismatic people can be extraordinarily persuasive — as long as the recipients of the persuasion remain in constant contact with the charismatic individual.

To be fairly sure that the attitude change will endure without having to maintain the constant contact or exact context of the persuasion situation, it is necessary to increase the likelihood that the receiver will elaborate (favorably) upon the argument which has been presented.

How can a persuader increase the likelihood of elaboration? First of all, the *motivation* to elaborate is important (Petty & Cacioppo, 1981). If the person being persuaded perceives the issue to be personally relevant and is involved in the issue, then elaboration is more likely (Petty & Cacioppo, 1981; Chaiken, 1980). The degree to which the message is discrepant (Petty & Cacioppo, 1979), the argument quality and quantity (Petty & Cacioppo, 1984), and the communication modality (Chaiken &

Eagly, 1983) have also been found to be important to the motivation of the receiver to elaborate upon the argument. Also, some people may enjoy thinking or actually need to think more about an argument; this has been called the "need for cognition" (Cacioppo & Petty, 1982; Cacioppo, Petty, & Morris, 1983).

There are some aspects of the situation that affect the individual's ability to elaborate on an argument. The message often needs to be repeated (Cacioppo & Petty, 1979), the message must be comprehensible (Eagly, 1974), and there must be few or no distractions (Petty, Wells, & Brock, 1976).

Finally, there are some characteristics of the receiver, apart from motivation, disposition, and perception of the situation, which seem to affect whether he/she will engage in elaboration. Intelligent individuals may process arguments more than less intelligent individuals. Those with a more internal locus of control — that is, those who see themselves as controlling their own behavior rather than being controlled by the environment — are more likely to elaborate on arguments. Finally, those people with high self-esteem are more likely to elaborate upon an argument than those with low self-esteem (Eagly, 1981).

The ELM model holds great promise for understanding the influence process in counseling; hopefully, this research will continue to be vigorous.

Client Variables in the Counseling Research

Although Strong (1968) and Strong and Matross (1973) included client variables in their model of social influence in counseling, very little research on the client variables mentioned followed. Perhaps this is because the client variables these authors mentioned — client involvement (Strong, 1968) and client need (Strong & Matross, 1973) — were not as firmly based on a research literature as were the counselor variables of expertness, attractiveness, and trustworthiness.

Strong and Matross (1973) theorized that clients would change attitudes in counseling when counselor social power and the client's need for the counselor's resources were greater than client resistance and opposition. Client need has been operationalized in a variety of ways by researchers.

Heppner and Dixon (1978) defined need as dissatisfaction with an emotional state, behavior, or situation. Dixon and Claiborn (1980) used a self-report of need (a request for help) as well as a stated pre-commitment to change the dissatisfying behavior. Sutton and Dixon (1983) combined client characteristics, such as problem-solving ability and self-efficacy with problem characteristics such as problem severity and time urgency, in their definition of client need. These studies seemed to support the idea that client need affects the success of the influence attempt in *some* ways. For example, Dixon and Claiborn found that commitment to change (but *not* self-report of need) had an effect on completion of tasks assigned by the counselor (but not on attitude change). In a study by Heppner and Dixon (1978) using perceived need, client need did not affect the counselor's ability to influence the client. Clearly, more research is needed to penetrate this confusion.

Client Expectations

What clients expect to get from counseling may affect their ultimate persuasibility. If a client's experience of counseling is congruent with expectations, then he/she may be more easily influenced. Client's expectations about counseling have definitely had an impact on how long they persist in treatment (Baekland & Lundwall, 1975). Tinsley, Workman, and Kass (1980) have developed an "Expectations About Counseling" questionnaire in order to operationalize this variable. The EAC has 135 items comprising 17 client expectations. Tinsley and his colleagues learned, through a factor analysis of scores on the EAC, that client expectations seemed to be made up of three separate factors: client personal commitment to counseling, expectations that the counselor-facilitative conditions would be present, and expectations that the counselor would be expert. Two of these factors have nice parallels with counselor "power bases" — expectations about counselor-facilitative conditions can be met through the counselor's attractive or "referent" behaviors and expectations about expertness by the counselor's expert behaviors. Theoretically, client expectations should be importantly related to the client's persuasibility and the outcome of the counselor's influence attempts. Kerr et al. (1983) used two different instruments to measure what they believed to be two distinct sets of client attitudes. One, a measure of "opposition," was essentially a measure of attitudes toward or expectations about the content of counseling — in this case, optimism or pessimism about career counseling. The second, a measure of "resistance," used an old instrument in a new way. The Counselor Rating Form (Barak & Lacrosse, 1975) had always been used after counseling to measure clients' perceptions of counselor's expertness, attractiveness, and trustworthiness. Kerr and her colleagues used the CRF as a *pre-test* to measure anticipatory perceptions — or expectations—about the counselor. They found over the course of two studies support for their hypothesis that counselor attractiveness is more effective than counselor expertness in overcoming resistance (defined as negative perceptions of counselors) and counselor expertness more effective than attractiveness in overcoming opposition (defined as negative attitudes toward the content of career counseling). Therefore, it is possible to see this study as evidence in favor of the idea that the nature of client expectations directly affects the outcome of the influence process. Clearly, the area of client expectations is going to be a fruitful one for social influence research.

Client Characteristics

Are some clients just too thick-headed to be able to be influenced? Any counselor who has tried to be persuasive with a true schizoid or a yes-butting neurotic is tempted to believe this! Practitioners have used a variety of labels for very resistant, oppositional clients and for their actions. Fenichel (1945) described "character resistances." Levy (1963) associated client influencability with the ease with which the patient will accept alternative constructions of events different from the one he/she holds.

Given the frequency with which counselors come up against clients who seem to have constructed brick walls around their attitudes, it is amazing how little of the counseling research has been directed to this problem. Because there seems to be no measure of "thick-headedness," it is necessary to glean from outcome research some possibilities to explore in attempting to understand why some clients seem impervious to change.

Cognitive abilities seem to be related to compliance in counseling; clients with greater cognitive skills such as reasoning and problem solving may be more easily influenced to achieve the goals of counseling (Helbrun, 1982). Intelligence, as measured by IQ has not been found to be consistently related to successful outcome (Meltzoff & Kornreich, 1970).

Client self-efficacy, a concept developed by Bandura (1982) to describe a client's perception of his or her own effectiveness as a problem solver, may have an important effect on client's influencability. If clients do not believe they are likely to be able to solve their problems, they are not likely to allow counselors to influence them.

Educational level seems to be related to successful outcome; more educated clients persist in therapy and have better outcomes (Garfield, 1978). The research relating other client characteristics to change in counseling is contradictory and complex. Age and sex do not seem to be important predictors of outcome (Garfield & Afflect, 1959). Psychiatric diagnosis has not been linked to persistence, although certain personalities such as schizoids and sociopaths do seem to be more impervious to change (Garfield & Afflect, 1959). Social class affects acceptance into and duration of counseling, but it is doubtful that social class is actually linked to influencability (Luborsky et al., 1971). Therefore, some nice, clean studies that precisely relate each of these client variables to persuasibility are especially needed.

Implications

The implications of the literature reviewed here for future research have been spelled out along the way. Counseling psychologists need to relate the social psychological research on receiver variables to research on client variables, and they need to do this as neatly as Strong and his colleagues extrapolated from communicator variables to counselor variables. Counseling psychologists need to jump into cognitive processes research with both feet if they wish to take advantage of the exciting new findings of this field. Finally, the research within the counseling literature on client variables is in a primitive state, and client needs, expectations, and characteristics related to influencability must become the focus of social influence research which has emphasized counselor variables too much.

But what about the implications of this review for the practitioner who cannot wait for the research to get in gear? The research areas explored here have many applications which can tentatively be made to the work of the counselor.

If there is one thing that can be said with certainty after this review, it is that the days of one-size-fits-all counselor are over. The idea that the same strategies can be used to influence all clients is simply not justified when clients vary in their susceptibility to persuasion (individually and situationally) and they vary from one situation to another in the degree to which they are likely to follow the central or peripheral route to attitude change.

Therefore, counselors need to tailor their strategies to their clients, rather than clinging to a theoretical position and pursuing blindly the techniques of that school, and they need to consider which techniques are most likely to enhance the client's persuasibility and the probability of elaboration at a particular point in time. Figure 1 at the conclusion of this chapter is a cautious step toward helping counselors with this tailoring process.

Figure 1

APPLYING THE RESEARCH ON CLIENT VARIABLES TO THE COUNSELING PROCESS

A. Assess a wide variety of client variables and consider how they will affect client persuasibility and elaboration likelihood.

-- Assess demographics; age, sex, social class, education level.
-- Assess client self-esteem, self-efficacy, cognitive skills and locus of control, "need for cognition."
-- Assess client perceived need.
-- Assess client expectations:
Anticipate the client's attitude toward the content of your persuasions.
Anticipate the amount of client's resistance to you as a counselor.

B. Set the stage for central rather than peripheral processing of your persuasion; but while backing yourself up with plenty of peripheral cues.
To maximize the elaboration likelihood:

-- Make sure the interpretations/arguments you use are personally relevant to the client.
-- Keep your message moderately discrepant.
-- Make sure your interpretations/arguments are not too long or too short.
-- Repeat your interpretations/arguments.
-- Be sure your interpretations/arguments are comprehensible.
-- Allow no distractions into the conversation.

Taking into account that the peripheral route may be taken, enhance the client's perceptions of your expertness, attractiveness, and trustworthiness.

C. Use situational strategies likely to enhance the client persuasibility.

-- Engage the client in active participation in the persuasion process by asking him/her to read your arguments/interpretations aloud or to role play as discrepant position.
-- Engage the client in making a public, behavioral commitment to change through a contract or statement before you and a group.
-- Try modifying the level of client's processing and persuasibility. Relaxation training and hypnosis can be used to decrease arousal; Gestalt and confrontation techniques can be used to heighten arousal.

D. Tailor your counseling strategies to what you have learned through your assessments. Clients with many of the characteristics related to noncompliance need high-power (that is high social-power) persuasions. Your use of social power cues and strategies can be more moderate with less resistant clients.

E. If your interpretations/arguments don't "take," if the client is not persuaded, start over again trying different strategies, until you hit the combination which makes it possible for your social power strategies to overcome the client's resistance and opposition and for change to occur. Try again the strategies aimed at enhancing the likelihood clients central processing of your arguments, so that change will be enduring.

CHAPTER 7

CLIENT RESISTANCE AND SOCIAL INFLUENCE

DAVID N. DIXON

SOCIAL INFLUENCE as an explanation of the counseling process was given major impetus by the seminal article of Strong (1968). This article suggested that counseling consisted of influencing client attitudes and behaviors to reach the goals of counseling. To accomplish this, the counselor first develops client perceptions of counselor expertness, attractiveness, and trustworthiness as well as enhances client commitment to change. Strong and Matross (1973) elaborated on this change process and proposed that client change as a result of counselor social power is a function of the client's perception of the congruence between counselor resources and client need. Subsequent research has focused on the counselor resources of expertness, attractiveness, and trustworthiness with little attention to client commitment to change or client need.

Despite the fact that both these articles saw counseling as a complex interpersonal influence situation, much of the resultant research has not captured the complexity of the counseling interaction. This research, as summarized by Corrigan et al. (1980) and Heppner and Dixon (1981), has focused narrowly both in terms of outcome variables and independent variables. The modal study has manipulated one of three counselor variables—expertness, attractiveness, and trustworthiness—and measured its effect on client perception of the counselor. In effect, few of these studies have looked at change in counseling at all. As Heppner and Dixon (1981) stated, "Many of these studies reviewed have little implication for theory. Those studies that focus on the perception of the counselor as the only dependent variable and fail to test the influence effects of the manipulated perceptions have few implications for dissonance theory

75

(Strong, 1968), attribution theory (Strong, 1971; Brehm, 1976), reactance theory (Brehm, 1976), or any other theory of interpersonal influence" (p. 547). To progress with social psychological research in counseling, a broader and more related set of independent and dependent variables needs to be considered.

One way to expand and invigorate the base for research on social influence in counseling is to look at related research literatures. Just as Goldstein, Heller, and Sechrest (1966), Strong (1968), and others did in taking those social psychological characteristics found to be related to persuasive communication and applying them to the counseling process, models found in related research areas may enrich social influence research. One area that shows promise for cross-fertilization is the concept of resistance, especially recent research on resistance coming from the more behavioral tradition. Whereas social influence has primarily focused on client compliance with counselor influence attempts, the resistance literature is primarily a documentation of failures of social influence or non-compliance with counselor influence efforts. Anderson and Stewart (1983) stated that, "Resistance to change in general and resistance to being influenced in particular always occur when individuals, groups, and systems are required by circumstances to alter their established behaviors" (p. 1). This chapter will first look at definitions of resistance and then provide a comprehensive model of resistance. Both tasks will be integrated with social influence research and theory.

Definitions of Resistance

Many definitions of resistance are available ranging from observable behaviors to implied dynamics underlying the behaviors. The next section will look at behaviors associated with resistance before looking at sources of resistance.

Observable Behaviors

Patterson (1982) identified two levels of resistance in treatment. Micro-level resistance is evidenced by client challenges, disagreements, disqualifications, and other negative client verbal responses to counselor attempts to influence the client. Resistance at the macro level is shown by client non-completion of homework assignments, missed appointments, and dropping out of treatment.

Jahn and Lichstein (1980) pointed out evidence of resistance in "the client who fails to provide self report data, never completes homework assignments, actively refrains from role playing, . . . and is unable or unwilling to discuss major personal problems. At the extreme of the resistance continuum is the client who drops out of therapy" (p. 304).

From a more cognitive orientation, resistance may primarily be evidenced by client non-acceptance of counselor cognitive explanations or by client refusal to reconceptualize the problem (Meichenbaum & Gilmore, 1982). From the analytic tradition, resistance while first being viewed intraphysically (Dixon et al., 1983), now includes an interactional perspective as well (Langs, 1980).

Regardless of orientation, the behaviors that lead to an assessment of resistive behaviors are focused on non-compliance or non-acceptance of counselor attempts to influence client behaviors and cognitions both in and out of the therapeutic environment.

Sources of Resistance

Munjack and Oziel (1978) have described five different types or sources of resistance. Type I resistance results from a lack of understanding by the client as to what is to be done. Type II resistance is due to a client's skill deficit; the client does not know how to implement the counselor's assignment. Type III resistance arises from lack of motivation or low expectations for success. Anxiety or guilt resulting from previous behavior or arising from counseling interactions characterizes Type IV resistance. Finally, Type V resistance arises from secondary gains associated with the symptoms.

Shelton and Levy (1981), drawing from the previous five categories (Munjack & Oziel, 1978), have given three inclusive reasons for treatment non-compliance. Type I resistance results when "the client lacks the necessary skills and knowledge to complete some or all of the tasks in the assignment." Type II resistance appears when "the client has cognitions that interfere with completion of the assignment." Finally, type III resistance arises when "the client's environment elicits non-compliance" (p. 39).

Strong and Matross (1973) also proposed multiple sources for treatment non-compliance called *restraining forces*. These forces were labeled *resistance* and *opposition*. Their use of the term "resistance" was more narrow than the use of the term throughout this chapter, with restraining forces being parallel to the more accepted, broad use of resistance. Resistance was defined by them as "forces aroused in the client that restrain acceptance of influence and are generated by the way the suggestion is stated and by the characteristics of the counselor stating it" (p. 26). Opposition on the other hand results from "forces that oppose the suggested changes and are generated by the characteristics and implications of the content of the suggestion" (pp. 26-27). Thus, non-compliance results from, in the first place, communicator or counselor style variables and, in the second, communication or content variables.

All of the authors have provided ways of differentiating sources of non-compliance or resistance. Resistance may result from a number of separate sources but probably is normally multiply determined, resulting from a number of the identified determinants.

Whereas the behaviors labeled as resistance cut across theories, the explanations (sources) of resistance vary from theory to theory. On the one hand, the analyst would attribute resistance to intrapsychic causes. The analyst sees resistance as functioning to protect the client from anxiety aroused by repressed unconscious materials. The analyst actively uses resistance in therapy, "since working through resistance *is* the therapy" (Anderson & Stewart, 1983). In comparison, the behaviorist would attribute resistance to failure of the behavior modifier to correctly design the behavior program. Behavioral techniques designed for resistance are primarily "ones which would serve to avoid the emergence of resistance" (Anderson & Stewart, 1983, p. 8). Meichenbaum and Gilmore (1982) stated that, "In cognitive-behavioral theories non-adherence to treatment plans is viewed not as a sign of a personality defect or a sign of stupidity on the part of the client, but instead as a natural consequence of an interfering thinking style, or a set of dysfunctional beliefs, and/or as the result of a set of interpersonal consequences that reinforce resistance" (p. 146). Thus, attributions of causality of resistance range from (a) stable client-dispositional attributes to (b) counselor-dispositional attributes to (c) unstable client-dispositional attributes and situational attributes.

It does seem useful to differentiate sources of resistant behaviors. On the one hand, the client may be unable to comply (e.g. skill deficits, lack of understanding), while in another situation the client may be unwilling to comply (e.g. conscious decision not to comply, secondary gains). Meichenbaum and Gilmore (1982) list the sources of problems for clients: (a) deficits in knowledge of what is appropriate, (b) inadequate skills to implement the appropriate coping behaviors, and (c) inhibition from acting due to doubt and fear. All of these would imply different treatment strategies to maximize the potential for client change. Meichenbaum and Gilmore stated that, "By matching the form of the intervention to the level of the client's competencies and to the nature of the deficit, one can avoid or minimize client resistance" (p. 142).

Comprehensive Model of Resistance

As stated earlier, the modal research study of social influence has examined only variables related to source credibility. Research in social psychology has long recognized the number of variables in the attitude change process. Zimbardo and Ebbeson (1970) described one model based on the sequence of "who says what to whom and with what effect." Major variables included are "communicator or source; communication or message; audience, recipients, or target population; and response dimensions" (p. 17). This more developed, although not new, way of viewing change seems needed in a model of resistance/social influence.

At least four components are related directly to resistance or treatment compliance. Included are: client characteristics and environments, problem characteristics, counselor attributes and behaviors, and intervention procedures. All of these components may directly impact on client change in counseling.

Client characteristics and environments include: client skills to follow through with treatment suggestions, general coping strategies, generalized expectations about therapeutic results, environment support systems, fixed modes of thinking or behaving, and demographic variables (Dixon et al., 1983). What the client brings to counseling as a result of genetic constitution, past history, and current conditions clearly impacts on the change process. These client characteristics and situations have largely been ignored by social influence researchers.

The second dimension, *problem characteristics*, or facilitating and/or restraining forces unique to a particular problem, are also important in understanding change. Granted, it is difficult to clearly separate client and problem characteristics. For example, expectations of change may relate to a client's general expectancy of change or may be specific to a particular problem. Differentiating these expectancies may prove difficult. Janis and Mann's (1977) *Conflict Model of Decision-Making* seems to be particularly relevant to guide research on problem characteristics. This model of decision making is an information-processing model applicable to decisions regarding all choices having real consequences (Dixon et al., 1983). For a client to engage in effective decision making, the decision must (a) have sufficient problem severity, (b) have a favorable gains-loss ratio, (c) have an adequate expectancy for change, and (d) allow sufficient time for deliberation.

Problem severity refers to the client's perception of the risks involved if no change occurs. If insufficient risks are perceived for not changing, then problem severity is assessed as minimal and the status quo is maintained. Gains-loss ratio introduces secondary gains or losses associated with the problem. When perceived gains outweigh losses, need for change will be high. Expectancy for change is the third dimension. When a client is unable to see alternatives that are better solutions than the current situation, need for change will be low. Finally, if a client perceives that a reasonable amount of time for change is available in counseling, stress remains controllable. When the four problem characteristics are optimal, a moderate level of stress is experienced by the client. If one or more of the characteristics is absent or perceived as negative, levels of stress will be respectively too low to involve the client in change or too high, blocking effective involvement.

Research looking at related variables and looking at treatment completion as an outcome measure include studies by Billings and Dixon (1984), Lochman and Brown (1980), and Sutton and Dixon (1986). Lochman and Brown (1980) and Sutton and Dixon (1986) found parents completing parent education workshops rated themselves higher in pre-treatment perceived need for change than those parents dropping out of treatment. Based on the conflict model (Janis & Mann, 1977), it could be assumed that a moderate level of stress was present with those parents who completed the treatment, while those with lower levels dropped out based on inadequate commitment to change or perceived need. In a study directly based on the model of Janis and Mann, Billings and Dixon (1984) assessed all four problem characteristics and examined their effects on three outcomes (workshop completion, homework completion, and workshop evaluation) in a parent training situation. Sets of variables from the four factors identified by Janis and Mann (1977) predicted workshop completion and workshop evaluation using stepwise discriminant analysis procedures.

The third dimension related to resistance is *counselor attributes and behaviors* that have been the focus of considerable research (Kerr, Claiborn, & Dixon, 1982). Counselor variables of expertness, attractiveness, and trustworthiness have all been associated with attitudinal and behavioral compliance (usually with analogue clients), but the nature of the relationship of each variable to the change process and the relationship among variables is unclear (Dixon et al., 1983).

Finally, the fourth dimension, *intervention procedures,* is by definition directly related to influence and change. Research on the delivery of interpretations (Claiborn, 1982; Levy, 1963), use of contracting (Dixon & Claiborn, 1981) and other behavioral-compliance procedures (Shelton &

Levy, 1981), and procedures designed to take advantage of reactance and resistance (Rohrbaugh, Tennen, Press, & White, 1982) all show specific promise for addressing the resistance phenomenon in counseling. A number of additional strategies for intervention show promise for overcoming resistance. The general concept of client involvement seems to be supported by social psychological research. Zimbardo and Ebbeson (1970) characterize the following conclusion: "Active participation is more effective in changing attitudes than passive exposure to persuasive communication. . . [as] . . . the most reliable in the area of attitude change" (p. 57). Client involvement is generally increased if care is taken to insure that the client understands the rationale and goal of each assignment. In fact, Shelton and Ackerman (1974) identified lack of explicit instructions and lack of relevance of the task as the two most common reasons for noncompliance with homework. Of course, whether an intervention is presented and perceived as sufficiently potent to bring about change directly relates to the third aspect of Janis and Mann's model, Expectancy for Change.

Implications for Research

Four independent variable domains emerge as important to resistance: client characteristics, problem characteristics, counselor attributes, and counseling interventions. These all impact on outcome and process measures (e.g. macro-micro level indices of behavior from Patterson, 1982) of resistance as treatment-relevant dependent variables. Preferably, research should consider four domains, broadly derived from social psychology, that are causally related to relevant outcomes.

Social influence research to date has been woefully lacking in the relevance of the dependent variables chosen. Dorn (1984) pointed out that the "degree to which the counselor is successful in influencing a client can be, and should be, assessed by quantifying the various behaviors the client engages in after each session or following termination" (p. 113). Corrigan et al. (1980) suggested that research focused on social influence in initial or early sessions could profitably "employ dependent measures of events such as return for a second interview, subjective expectations of assistance, or expressed confidence in the counselor" (p. 427).

Four studies of early premature termination in counseling provide examples for improved dependent measures in social influence research (Betz & Shullman, 1979; Billings & Dixon, 1984; Epperson, Bushway, &

Warman, 1983; Krauskopf, Baumgarden, & Mandracchia, 1981). All studies examined early premature termination or client return rate as a meaningful outcome measure of resistance/social influence. Variables related to return rate included sex of intake counselor (although not in a consistent manner), counselor-client agreement on problem definition, and measures of problem characteristics derived from Janis and Mann (1977). These studies illustrate incorporation of useful outcome measures with conceptually meaningful predictor variables.

A summary of elements of a comprehensive model of resistance/ social influence can be seen in Table 7-1.

TABLE 7-1

COMPREHENSIVE MODEL OF RESISTANCE/SOCIAL INFLUENCE

These incoming conditions (A) ------ interacting with these (B) ----➤ result in (C) treatment conditions

A.1 Client Characteristics:
  a. skills
  b. general coping strategies
  c. generalized expectations
  d. modes of thinking/ behaving
  e. environmental support
  f. demographic variables

B.1 Counselor Attributes and Behaviors
  a. expertness
  b. attractiveness
  c. trustworthiness

C.1 Compliance = Social Influence

2 Problem Characteristics:
  a. problem severity
  b. gains-loss ratio
  c. expectancy for change
  d. time urgency

2 Intervention Procedures:
  a. rationale/context
  b. change strategy
  c. involvement

2 Noncompliance = Resistance

One ethical issue often not addressed in influence research in counseling is that of the positive aspects of resistance. Clearly, it is a positive sign for a client to resist ill-defined and poorly explained assignments. Meichenbaum and Gilmore (1982) asserted that, "It is necessary for us as therapists to assure the efficacy of a treatment before we start ensuring compliance" (p. 154). Further, resistance as an additional source of information about the client, the problem, the counselor, and the treatment strategy should not be precluded. Anderson and Stewart (1983) illustrated the positive aspects of resistance: "Without a certain amount of resistance to being influenced, families and individuals would be converted by every medicine man, commercial, or talk show expert that happened to bend their collective ear. Resistance . . . can be a sign of good health and good judgment" (p. 4).

In conclusion, it seems productive to bridge the research in resistance with social psychological research in counseling. The resistance literature (especially the behavioral explanations) provides a useful set of outcome measures, and the interpersonal influence literature provides a rich source of predictor variables. This combination provides a base for viewing change and resistance to change in a complex, yet meaningful, useful manner.

The chapter has outlined some specific components of a model for research that includes client characteristics, problem characteristics, counselor attributes, and counselor interventions as predictors of resistant behaviors such as early premature termination, non-completion of homework, and process measures of perceptions of counselor. There is a great need for further definition of these variables and development of measures for these dimensions. Research in social influence will be strengthened by consideration of a more comprehensive set of variables associated with influence/resistance and by assessing this impact using dependent variables of relevance to counseling.

CHAPTER 8

LANGUAGE USE AND SOCIAL INFLUENCE IN COUNSELING

NAOMI M. MEARA AND
MICHAEL J. PATTON

> "Sticks and stones are hard on bones.
> Aimed with angry art,
> Words can sting like anything.
> But silence breaks the heart."
>
> Phyllis McGinley

THIS BIT OF whimsical verse illustrates the close relationship between words and their likely impact on others. More fundamentally, however, the verse illustrates how the poet's particular use of words is intertwined with the meaning that those words have for us. As adult readers of the English language, we know what the poet has in mind by our recognizing how she is using the words to express her point.

For example, we recognize that when she says "words can sting like anything but silence breaks the heart," she is speaking metaphorically. If we are unable to understand metaphor, we could not appreciate the meaning of most poetry or to understand what the poet means to convey. Our recognition that the poet is using words metaphorically on this occasion is a critical component of the meaning they have for us. Thus, to completely understand what someone is saying, it is essential that we understand how they are using words.

In using language, we take for granted or trust that others understand not only the words we use but recognize how we are using them.

Our knowledge as interpreters of the countless ways in which persons speak and write allows their speeches and written documents to convey meaning, and provides for the possibility that through language usage we can influence each other.

Counseling is an example of a social occasion in which the language practices of the participants provide for the possibility that the conversation will effect one or both of them. With their use of language, the participants create, sustain, or change their social and interpersonal realities. For a number of years we and our colleagues (Patton & Meara, forthcoming; Pepinsky, 1985; Pepinsky & Patton, 1971) have argued that the natural language practices of persons are primary methods for organizing counselor and client experience and formulating desired treatment outcomes (Meara, et al., 1981). Our contention is that with the use of recognizable practices of speaking (or writing), one person conveys meaning to and is able to influence another. For us as counselors, then, an answer to the question of how language influences the work we do is to be provided by a description of how counseling participants use language.

Since Strong's (1968) provocative paper on social influence, and the ensuing work (cf. Corrigan et al., 1980; Heppener & Dixon, 1980), it has been widely accepted that social influence is an important way of talking about events in counseling. Our purpose here is to discuss our efforts related to understanding psychological treatment based on our conceptualizations of social influence and language use. In this discussion we ask the reader to keep in mind that the constructs and ideas we present represent our construction of the counseling process and our views that (a) language use molds the mutual influence attempts and accomplishments of counselor and client, and (b) evidence of these attempts and accomplishments can be inferred from studying counselor and client language patterns. Our work can be characterized as attempts to conceptualize, describe and if possible eventually explain how language use influences interactive discourse and, secondarily, how language use by participants in interactive discourse is the exercise of social influence.

To begin to address these questions, we and our colleagues have developed a *Computer-Assisted Language Analysis System* (CALAS) which provides primitive yet basic information regarding some stylistic and semantic attributes of natural language discourse (Rush et al., 1974; Meara, 1976; Pepinsky 1974, 1985; Pepinsky et al., 1977). The rationale for developing a language analysis system and its applications to date are based on earlier theorizing and empirical investigations, most notably Pepinsky and Karst (1964) and Pepinsky and Patton (1971). These authors articulated the importance of social influence (Pepinsky & Karst, 1964) and developed an interactive definition of psychological treatment (Pepinsky & Patton 1971). This view of psychological treatment formed the basis for a still-developing model of client-counselor interaction and change (Patton, Fuhriman & Bieber, 1977; Pepinsky 1974, 1985; Pepinsky & DeStefano, 1983). From this work came further development and comments regarding how language conveys meaning (Patton & Meara, forthcoming), phenomenological conceptualizations of the management of social interaction in counseling and specific empirical work investigating language patterns in interactive discourse.

The work of Cook (1979) and other case grammarians provided the linguistic foundation for our speculations about the use of language in interactive discourse and for the technical construction of the CALAS. The *Matrix Model of Case Grammar* is articulated fully by Cook (1979), and our adaptation of the model is explicated by Meara (1983), Meara et al. (1981) and more recently and thoroughly by Pepinsky (1985).

A central question of our research endeavors has been to what extent, if at all, can linguistic units of measure inform us about the progress of the interaction. To address this question, we and others have looked at several language patterns displayed by the participants within discourse that we believe reflect the presence of mutual social influence and may be a prelude to and/or indicative of substantive concerted actions and influence accomplishments that we believe to be necessary for effective psychological treatment.

These patterns include (a) tracking, (b) convergence, (c) discussion topics, (d) sequences, and (e) comments. *Convergence* is a term used by Pepinsky and Karst (1964) in explaining how social influence is exerted in therapy. We use the term here to denote the convergence or simultaneous display of specific language patterns or grammatical structures used by participants in interactive discourse. Tracking (cf. Jaffee, 1964) is defined as one participant, usually the less influential, modeling or imitating the language displays of the other. In convergence, participants may begin with dissimilar patterns and converge on one pattern that is different from the pattern with which either began. In tracking, one participant does not change language pattern significantly; the other's patterns become more similar to the first.

Discussion topics refer to content and have less to do with language structure. We hypothesize that when counselor and client show preference for the same discussion topic, common understanding is present in the interaction. Sequences refer to the probabilities associated with the occurrence of specific responses of one participant following the specific responses of the other. Sequences can refer to topics, structure, or categories such as those found in the work of Friedlander and Phillips (1984). For example, if a client is pursuing a topic the counselor believes to be appropriate, the counselor is more likely to respond with what Friedlander (1984) labels a "passing turn" (e.g. "yes," "go on") than to introduce a new topic (in Friedlander's terms a "topic shift initiation"). Sequencing is particularly important in the work of Lichtenberg and Hummel (1976) and Friedlander (1984). It seems to us that any method of categorizing participant responses, such as Hill's *Counselor and Client Verbal Response Modes Category Systems* (cf. Hill, 1983) has potential for providing information about how social influence is being exerted and displayed in the interaction, if the patterns of sequencing are investigated.

Language Use, Social Influence and Units of Measure

As is well known, one of the classic problems in psychological research is determining units of measure. Since social scientists are evaluating constructs rather than physical objects, researchers are often confronted with the task of operationalizing the constructs into procedures that can be observed and counted. In addition, the units chosen must have some logical connection to the construct being evaluated so that inferences can be made about the nature of the construct by studying the results of the measurements. We are faced with these problems as we seek to develop linguistic units to measure hypothesized variables of psychological treatment.

CALAS can be described as a computerized algorithm for operationalizing into grammatical constructions some elements in the structures of two methods of using words: (a) naming and (b) relating. From these grammatical constructions we have derived semantic and stylistic measures, which provide us with information about participant language patterns, and from which we make inferences about the progress of the interaction, and about other phenomena related to psychological treatment, such as intentionality, concerted action and social influence.

Much of our research to date has been based upon our ability to operationalize, via the CALAS, elements in the structure of the concept of relating. This accomplishment is based on our adapting (Meara et al.,

1981; Pepinsky, 1985) of Cook's (1979) matrix model of case grammar and then creating the appropriate algorithms for the development of the computer programs.

Patton and Meara (forthcoming) explain case grammar, the CALAS and the derived units of measure in detail. Briefly, case grammar classifies the structures of natural language according to the semantic relationship between what are traditionally called nouns and verbs (Reed, 1983). As Patton and Meara (forthcoming) note:

> The Matrix Model of Case Grammar postulates that there are essential and inherent semantic relations (such as state, process or action) in the deep structure of English language. It is the person's use of these standardizing relations that render language meaningful in the first two dimensions (i.e., naming and relating) . . . . In particular [this model] provides an excellent tool to investigate the second dimension of language use, that of relating named things. Simply from a case grammar perspective the named things are noun phrases and the relators are verb phrases. . . . These descriptions constitute a metalanguage which we use to characterize and measure semantic attributes of informative displays.

Attributes of style, or stylistics, constitute a second set of derived measures. Stylistics is thought to be more representative of the "surface structure" of language and has more to do with the manner in which something is said rather than what was intended. We used the concept of the clause to operationalize our notion of stylistics. In addition to the clause we have used other grammatical units to measure style, such as words and phrases (e.g. cf. Hurndon, Pepinsky, & Meara, 1979). By means of these semantic and stylistic units, discourse can be described and compared across such things as speakers, topics, or segments.

Research and Implications

Our empirical work has been directed toward investigating the role of language in various components of psychological treatment. Specifically we have investigated selected linguistic attributes, and Patton and Meara (forthcoming) provide a thorough review of all that research to date. Here, we review a few studies that we believe are directly relevant to and have implications for further research in the areas of social influence and language use in counseling.

For purposes of discussion, we have divided our studies into two categories. The first contains studies related to the question of how social influence is exerted through language. All of the studies in this group are characterized by specific interventions (what we might term "recognized" social influence attempts) which are then measured and described linguistically. The second category consists of studies that address the question of how social influence is displayed through language. This second group describes selected occasions of psychological treatment in terms of the semantic and stylistic properties of client and counselor language usage. From these descriptions inferences are made about what psychological events or phenomena (in this case those related to social influence) might be present in the interaction.

Hurndon, Pepinsky and Meara (1979), using Hunt's *Paragraph Completion Method,* found that those who used complex language as measured by verbal productivity were judged to have a higher conceptual level than those who used simple language. Hector, Wyman and Meara (1984) designed a study to provide a direct test of the effect of language on perceived social influence. Specifically, they investigated how selected semantic and stylistic variables generated by the CALAS, and used by a counselor in an analogue counseling session, affected subjects' perceptions of the counselor's social influence as measured by the CRF (Barak & LaCrosse, 1975). The counselor's language was manipulated so that there were four experimental conditions: language use classified as (a) state simple, (b) action simple, (c) state complex, and (d) action complex. The results showed that the only effect on the dependent measures (i.e. expertness, attractiveness, and trustworthiness) was that the subjects perceived the counselor as more expert in the complex language conditions than in the simple language conditions.

Complex language is a stylistic variable and does seem to influence perceptions of expertness or intellectual ability. We must exercise caution in generalizing these findings, but these results seem similar to Schmidt and Strong's (1970) work which found an inverse relationship between amount of counselor training and/or experience and the level of expertness assigned to them by students from introductory psychology courses.

Reed, Hector and Meara (1984) replicated the work of Hector et al. (1984) using what they termed "a more sophisticated population." Their subjects were graduate students who had had some instruction in counseling. With this population, none of the stylistic or semantic variables had any effect upon the subjects' perceived social influence of the counselor as measured by the dimensions of the CRF.

Several issues seem important here. First of all, the studies that report positive results do so for only stylistic measures and for dimensions that could roughly be labelled expertness and relate to samples drawn from college students. The fact that, as yet, there are no positive results related to semantic measures or to other dimensions of social influence is of concern. It seems, too, that samples drawn from populations that have some knowledge of counseling are not "taken in" by what we might term expert jargon.

Wycoff et al. (1982) compared the linguistic patterns of counselors who were judged to be high empathic responders (HERS) with those of counselors who were judged to be low empathic responders (LERS). Counselors use empathy to influence the interaction in a number of ways, including building the relationship and encouraging client self-disclosure. The results of this study indicated that from a stylistic perspective the LERS were more verbally productive and, from a sematic perspective, they used more action verb phrases than the HERS. Contrary to predictions, however, there were no differences on other measures of stylistic complexity or in the use of state verb phrases. The authors suggest that counselors could be trained to be more skillful in empathic responding if they were trained to use language patterns typical of high empathic responders.

Our second category of studies, which deals with the question of how social influence is displayed in language, simply addresses from the opposite perspective. Instead of taking "established" phenomena and explicating what they look like linguistically, we are taking linguistic phenomena and inferring what is happening in interactive discourse. The studies in this category include: Bieber, Patton and Fuhriman (1977), Bieber (1978), Meara, Shannon and Pepinsky, (1979), Meara et al. (1981), and Patton, Fuhriman and Bieber (1977). They have been reviewed extensively elsewhere (Patton & Meara, forthcoming; Pepinsky, 1985) and will be briefly summarized below.

The studies by Bieber et al. (1977), Bieber (1978), and Patton et al. (1977) drew their data from the same set of counselor and client interviews. The data set was three different pairs of clients and counselors, two from a university counseling center and one from a comprehensive community mental health center. The first, eleventh and twenty-fifth interviews in each series were analyzed via an earlier version of the CALAS.

Each of the studies concentrated on different language features. The results were taken as evidence for the presence of social influence via tracking and convergence, and the authors inferred the presence of common understanding. For example, in concentrating on the verb phrase, the major semantic relator, Patton et al. (1977) found in one of the counselor-client pairs changes in the variations and frequency of verb types across the three interviews. These changes were similar for both participants in amount and direction of change. Bieber et al. (1977) conducted a more thorough analysis of this same counselor and client pair and noted that the client had increased her references to self as an experiencer by the end of the twenty-fifth interview. Finally, Bieber (1978), using all three counselor-client pairs, not only found evidence for tracking and convergence via the language but found that the two pairs with the client-centered counselors had a different pattern of language usage than the pair with the psychoanalytically oriented counselor. In general, the language was in accord with what one would expect knowing the treatment methods and goals of these two different theoretical orientations. From these results the authors concluded that there was common understanding concerning what were later termed as treatment policies (Meara et al., 1981).

The Meara et al. (1979, 1981) studies also used a common data set: excerpts from the well-known "Gloria" films (Shostrom 1966). In the first study, stylistic variables were studied via the CALAS and in the second, semantic ones. The results of the first study indicated that all three counselors, Rogers, Perls and Ellis, were significantly different from one another across four dependent measures of stylistic complexity; and again, as noted above in the Bieber et al. (1977) and Patton et al. (1977) work, these differences were according to what one might expect, knowing the orientations of the therapists. Perhaps the most striking result, and from which the authors inferred the presence of social influence, was the fact that the language patterns of the client, Gloria, were significantly different in all three interviews, and that they were similar to the therapist with whom she was working at the time.

In the second study (Meara et al., 1981) there were again differences among the therapists on the semantic measures but these differences did not seem to influence Gloria's semantic language patterns. The latter result is in accord with Bieber et al. (1977), who noted that clients are not influenced to change their semantic displays in initial interviews but may be influenced to do so in later interviews.

All the studies in the second category rely heavily on inference. They are based on an assumption that language use is indicative of cognitive processes such as intention and interpretation and that persons can and do use language to convey what they mean. This area of inquiry might prove fruitful in attempting to establish concurrent validity of some of psychology's measures of social influence and other psychological phenomena thought to be present in counseling. For example, if inferences we make about a counseling session derived from other measures of social influence are similar to inferences we make about that same counseling session from a language analysis, we can have more assurance that the hypothesized construct we are attempting to analyze (in this case social influence) has a practical observability across different methods of inquiry. In addition, if we know about specific language patterns and their effect on an interaction, we can use this information in training.

The results of the studies in the second category support the initial proposition by Pepinsky and Karst (1964) that psychotherapy is an "interactional process in which the client acquires a psychological grammar made available . . . by the therapist" (p. 335). It stands to reason that the more counselors and clients know about this grammar and how to use it, the more effective psychological treatment can be.

Summary

We have maintained that language use is a powerful method of social influence. We have demonstrated how a model of language usage based on case grammar elements can provide the basis for generating semantic and stylistic measures that can be applied to evaluating language patterns of interactive discourse. We have reviewed briefly exploratory research that we contend holds promise in demonstrating how (a) social influence is exerted through language and (b) how social influence is displayed through language. We think that the implications of this work are that by pursuing linguistic lines of inquiry we can better understand the construct of social influence and other phenomena of counseling, as well as learn more about how the work of counseling is accomplished.

CHAPTER 9

PHYSICAL ATTRACTIVENESS, SOCIAL INFLUENCES, AND COUNSELING PROCESSES

ALICE M. VARGAS AND JOHN G. BORKOWSKI

Introduction

PHYSICAL ATTRACTIVENESS is a dominant component in most social interchanges. It catches the eye, maintains attention in the face of distraction, or prompts sustaining behaviors even in socially stressful contexts. Little wonder that physical attractiveness plays an important role in counseling.

One of the first impressions that a client has of a counselor centers on his or her physical attractiveness. In a more subtle way, attractiveness is at the heart of a potentially important reciprocal relationship: the client may form impressions about the counselor, and the counselor's response style may be influenced by the client's attractiveness. In short, before a single word is exchanged between client and counselor, a reciprocal relationship, based on attractiveness, may develop and influence the long-term success or failure of the therapeutic process. Although perceptions about the therapist's physical characteristics will not sustain the counseling process in the long run, judgments about attractiveness may play a causal role in the client's emerging perceptions about expertness and trustworthiness—the more substantial features of Stage 1 processes in Strong's (1968) social influence model.

Based on Festinger's (1957) cognitive dissonance theory, Strong (1968) suggested that a counselor's attempts to change a client's actions or opinions encourages dissonance in the client. Dissonance can be re-

duced by clients in one of five ways: (a) by changing in the direction proposed by the counselor, (2) by discrediting the counselor, (3) by discrediting the issue, (4) by changing the counselor's opinion, or (5) by finding
others who agree with the client. Strong hypothesized that by reducing
the likelihood of the second and third alternatives, counselors enhance
the likelihood that the first alternative will occur. Extrapolating from research in social psychology, Strong suggested that the degree to which
counselors are perceived as expert, attractive, and trustworthy increases
the likelihood that the client will accept the counselor's views, since these
are communicator characteristics preventing the derogation of the communicator. The client will change his or her cognitive constructs in the
direction advocated by the counselor only if the other means of dissonance reduction are controlled. In addition, by increasing the client's involvement in counseling, the likelihood of minimizing the issue is
reduced. Based on hypotheses about dissonance reduction, Strong
formed a two-stage model of counseling. Initially, the counselor
enhances her perceived expertness, attractiveness, trustworthiness, and
the client's involvement in the first stage of counseling increases. In the
second stage, the counselor uses her influence to enhance opinion and/
or effect behavioral change in the client.

This review is concerned with one of the variables postulated by
Strong (1968) to be facilitative in the first stage of counseling —
counselor attractiveness. Strong asserted that perceived similarity to,
compatibility with, and liking for the counselor are the basis for clients'
perceptions of counselor attractiveness. Studies of perceived counselor
attractiveness have included: (a) behavioral cues such as self-disclosure
and nonverbal behavior; (b) reputational cues such as direct and trait
structuring; and (c) evidential cues such as physical attractiveness, setting, attire, sex, and race (Corrigan et al., 1980).

Although not included as a basis of attraction in Strong's (1968) original statement, physical attractiveness is one of the evidential cues that
has been consistently shown to influence interpersonal attraction and
performance evaluation. In addition, physical attractiveness becomes a
setting variable that interrelates with, and perhaps determines, major
judgments formed by the client about the counselor's sense of understanding, empathy, sincerity, and trustworthiness. It is these characteristics that effective counselors possess, or attempt to emulate, and it is
these attributes of effective counseling that may be directly influenced
by perceptions about physical attractiveness. Although it is disconcerting to some to suggest that the attractiveness of a therapist might

enhance or hinder the development of essential Stage 1 processes, the data base that we review in the next section suggests that initial judgments about the counselor's physical features do indeed influence the client's judgments about expertness and trustworthiness as the therapeutic process unfolds.

Research on Physical Attractiveness and Counseling Processes

The work of Cash and colleagues forced us to recognize the importance of physical attractiveness in determining the course of subsequent counseling processes (Cash et al., 1975; Cash & Kehr, 1978). In comparison with an unattractive counselor, an attractive counselor was generally perceived more favorably by clients of both sexes, being judged as more assertive, warm, competent, and trustworthy. Relevant to the long-term success of therapy, clients who had an attractive therapist were also more optimistic about the future course of therapeutic events and had more positive outcome expectancies for the resolution of their problems. Cash and Kehr (1978) suggested the impact of attractiveness manipulations in past research may have been due more to the debilitative influence of unattractiveness rather than the facilitative influence of attractiveness. This hypothesis has not received confirmation in more recent research that was aimed at unraveling the interactive effects of physical attractiveness and counseling skills on outcomes.

In a series of studies (Vargas & Borkowski, 1982, 1983), we have attempted to address several major methodological problems that have surfaced in past research on physical attractiveness: past analogues to real-life counseling situations have been artificial (e.g. ratings taken after a single brief therapeutic session) and/or the attractiveness variable has not been manipulated so as to reflect reliable representations of attractive and unattractive therapists. The analogue design of our studies attended to these methodological shortcomings and allowed us to search for the interaction between quality of counseling skills — defined by the presence or absence of empathy, genuineness, and positive regard — and physical attractiveness as co-determinants of counseling effectiveness.

Basically, we used a simulation procedure in which small groups of college students saw either an attractive or unattractive counselor who exhibited either good counseling skills, as defined by the person-centered approach of Rogers (1951), or poor counseling skills. The counselor-client relationship unfolded as a female therapist interacted on a videotape with a young man who had major concerns about his deficient social skills. The initial study of Vargas and Borkowski (1982) was essentially a 2 × 2 × 2 × 2 design in which the between-subjects variables were counseling skills (good and poor), physical attractiveness (attractive or unattractive), number of ratings (after Sessions 1 and 3 or after Session 3 only), and actress (two actresses served as a replication variable). To determine the effect of attractiveness and counseling skills on the process of counseling, the students were asked to assume the role of the client and to participate in three counseling sessions over a period of three consecutive days, with measures of the counselor's effectiveness taken after the first and/or third sessions. Following the third session, a measure of expectations of the counselor's potential effectiveness in dealing with other types of problems was also recorded.

In contrast to previous research on physical attractiveness, the present study simultaneously manipulated physical attractiveness and the quality of counseling skills as a female counselor treated a male's social skills problem during three sessions. The analogue design was unique in attempting to assess ongoing impressions of the therapist's attractiveness and her degree of effectiveness (defined in terms of sincerity and trustworthiness) after an intake session and/or after therapy had progressed. Since adult males role-played the observed client interacting with the same female counselor during three sessions, our simulation procedure was more similar to the actual counseling process than prior research, which generally has focused on a single, brief counseling session. Also, unlike some previous studies (Carter, 1978; Lewis & Walsh, 1978), the attractiveness manipulation was highly successful, involving widely discrepant ratings (by pilot subjects of the same age as the actual subjects) at the extremes of the attractiveness scales for each therapist.

Multivariate analysis showed significant main effects for physical attractiveness and for counseling skills. The effects due to attractiveness were strong, accounting for more than 50% of the variance in the dependent measures of effectiveness. No interaction between attractiveness and counseling skills was observed. These results suggest that both skilled and unskilled counselors received an added boost in terms of their perceived effectiveness in the early part of Stage 1 if they are attractive. This interpretation is important because it identified a causal variable, physical attractiveness, that influences counseling outcomes through the attributes of trustworthiness, sincerity, empathy, and positive regard.

It is important to note that four of the five dependent measures in the multivariate analysis involved rating the counselor's past performance (i.e. her therapeutic effectiveness). In contrast, the dependent measure that elicited judgments of future competency in new therapy situations yielded a significant univariate interaction between the quality of counseling skills and the degree of physical attractiveness. When the counselor had poor skills, attractiveness made little difference. Clients simply did not want to receive further treatment from ineffective counselors. If the counselor had good skills, however, then attractiveness added to judgments about her desirability as a counselor in new therapeutic settings that might be encountered in the client's immediate future.

It appears then that physical attractiveness has a "lingering" or prolonged influence on Stage 2 processing. This conclusion, based on the univariate analysis of future expectancy data, is supported by the positive correlation in the good skills conditions between early judgments of attractiveness and later judgments about future expectancies. Given that the counselor had good skills, students who were initially impressed by her attractiveness rated her more favorably on the future expectancies measure than clients who made lower initial judgments about the attractiveness of the counselor. Good counseling skills seem to be augmented by clients' initial judgments about perceived physical attractiveness, at least in terms of our future expectancies measure, an assessment of the clients' intentions to remain in therapy.

The same conclusion cannot be drawn about the impact of an attractive therapist on future expectancies when she is unskilled. In this situation, attractiveness has little positive influence on future expectancies judgments. In fact, the negative correlation between early judgments of attractiveness and later judgments of expectancy and effectiveness in the poor skills condition suggest that attractiveness can be detrimental to the counseling process if therapeutic skills are judged low in quality.

In the next set of studies, Vargas and Borkowski (1983) assessed the importance of the physical attractiveness of a counselor in combination with various facets of client attractiveness. The intent here was to observe whether the affects of physical attractiveness we observed in our initial study were attenuated by clients' perceived attractiveness about themselves or by inference about how highly they valued physical attractiveness in social interchange contexts. We conducted two analogue experiments, searching for the interaction between clients' physical attractiveness (or susceptibility to attractiveness) and the attractiveness of a female counselor as joint determinants of counseling effectiveness.

The first study in this series was essentially a 2 × 2 × 2 × 2 design in which the between-subjects variables were counselor attractiveness (attractive or unattractive), actress (two actresses played the role of the counselor and served as a replication factor), client attractiveness (moderately unattractive-very attractive), and sex of client. The other study was a 2 × 2 × 2 design in which the variables were counselor attractiveness (attractive or unattractive), actress (again two actresses played the role of the counselor), and client susceptibility to attractiveness (highly or moderately influenced by attractiveness). For a more complete description of the methods used to infer level of client susceptibility (from judgments made about the characteristics of unseen females based only on their voices), see Vargas and Borkowski (1983, p. 148). In these two studies, college students assumed the role of the client and viewed three counseling sessions, with measures of the counselor's effectiveness obtained after the third session.

In both experiments, the physical attractiveness of the counselor was a potent variable affecting the success of the counseling process. The physically attractive counselor was judged more effective and desirable in treating other potential mental health problems than the physically unattractive counselor. Furthermore, physical attractiveness of the counselor accounted for over 50% of the variance in all dependent measures, including perceived effectiveness. The strong influence of counselor attractiveness was maintained irrespective of the client's perceived physical attractiveness, sex, or susceptibility to attractiveness. It should be stressed, however, that these findings are limited to the context of client-centered therapy with a social skills problem.

These two experiments suggest that physical attractiveness gives the female therapist, treating both male and female clients, an advantage in terms of perceived effectiveness. In addition, clients viewed the attractive counselor more favorably in terms of future expectancies about the treatment of other mental health problems—an outcome that may have long-term consequences for Stage 2 processes. Based on assessments of the clients' intentions to remain with the therapist if other problems arise, we suspect that clients sometimes make early decisions about continuing in therapy based on "non-professional" reasons, such as feelings about the physical attractiveness of even a moderately skilled counselor.

Although the percentage of variance accounted for by the physical attractiveness of the counselor was equivalent for clients of both sexes, male clients attributed a higher overall level of skillfulness to the female counselors than did female clients. In addition, male clients were more optimistic about future counseling outcomes than the female clients. It should be noted that the client presented in the videotapes was male. This factor could account for some of the sex-related findings, especially if some female subjects had difficulty identifying with social skills problems of the male client. Indeed, interview data showed that female subjects had slightly more difficulty identifying with the client; this difference, however, was not significant. These sex-related findings are in line with previous research of Lewis and Walsh (1978), showing that responses by female clients to an attractive female counselor were positive but far less pronounced than responses elicited by an attractive male counselor in the Cash et al. (1975) study. The findings have implications for same-sex versus opposite-sex matches between clients and counselors—a topic we develop in the next section.

In the final experiment in this series, we assessed the importance of the susceptibility of male clients to the physical attractiveness of their female counselor in terms of their perceptions about therapeutic effectiveness. Susceptibility to attractiveness was defined by pretest judgments about the importance of physical attractiveness in dating situations together with attributions of physical attractiveness to audiotapes of unseen females. Even in this experiment, the physical attractiveness of the counselor was of paramount importance in determining counseling effectiveness. In fact, clients who were judged to be more susceptible to physical attractiveness gave lower ratings on future expectancy scales than clients less influenced by attractiveness. This effect was greatest when the counselor was attractive, suggesting that even though a client might adopt a neutral position about the importance of mere physical qualities, counselor attractiveness nevertheless can play a major role in the decision to continue in therapy—a role that is far greater than the client may realize.

Implications for Research, Theory, and Therapy

Social Influences and Attractiveness

The data presented here square with research in social psychology showing that attractive people of both sexes are expected to possess socially desirable personality traits. Attractive people are assumed to be competent and qualified (Dion, Berscheid, & Walster, 1972; Miller, 1970; Cash, Gillen, & Burns, 1977; Dipboye et al., 1975). Although the relationship between a client's expectations and therapeutic outcome is by no means direct and unequivocal (Wilkins, 1973), numerous authors have marshalled evidence showing that a client's outcome expectancies can be therapeutically facilitative (Frank, 1973; Friedman, 1973; Uhlenhuth & Duncan, 1968; Wilkins, 1971). Positive expectations are necessary conditions for the client's continuation in treatment and compliance with the therapist's interventions (Murray & Jacobson, 1971). Physical attractiveness seems to be one characteristic of the therapist that promotes positive client expectations, which in turn augment the first stage of the counseling process.

It would be interesting to study the reactions of male clients to male versus female counselors using the Vargas and Borkowski (1983) design, since it has been suggested that male clients rate male counselors lower than female clients (Carter, 1978). It might be hypothesized from past research (Carter, 1978; Cash et al., 1975; Lewis & Walsh, 1978; Vargas & Borkowski, 1983) that both males and females tend to be less critical of, or perhaps more positive toward, therapists of the opposite sex, thus maximizing the influence of the attractiveness manipulation.

Several studies in social psychology have analyzed the influence of attractiveness on dyadic relationships, finding evidence of a relationship between similarity of physical attractiveness and interpersonal attraction (Murstein, 1972; Murstein & Christy, 1974; Cash & Derlega, 1978). Vargas and Borkowski (1983) attempted to determine if a person's own level of physical attractiveness served as a moderating influence on the counseling process. The data suggested that, unlike research on interpersonal attraction, the attractiveness of both female and male clients in a counseling situation does not significantly influence perceptions and expectations of a female counselor. This conclusion has implications for matching in forming client-counselor dyads. It appears from our limited data-base that matching by level of attractiveness would not be particularly facilitative. Instead, both unattractive or attractive clients seem to prefer an attractive therapist, even one of the same sex.

Research to date on matching by virtue of sex is inconclusive, with some studies showing same-sex matching to be facilitative whereas others have not found an advantage to matching (Scher, 1975; Hoffman-Graff, 1977; Simons & Helms, 1976; Geer & Hurst, 1976). The literature on physical attractiveness and the therapy process has also been unclear as to whether same-sex matching is facilitative (Cash et al., 1975; Carter, 1978; Lewis & Walsh, 1978; Cash & Kehr, 1978). Simons and Helms (1976) and Hoffman-Graff (1977) have suggested that previous studies may have been too simplistic in their approach to studying the sex variable. Clients have often been asked merely to state a sex preference. This preference may not correspond to the actual choice made by a client in counseling settings or when counselor attractiveness is specified.

We have suggested that the study of gender in isolation from other variables is misleading. For instance, data reported in the Vargas and Borkowski (1983) study reflected the effects of gender differences in combination with physical attractiveness. The results suggested that it is appropriate to pair male or female clients with an attractive therapist of the same or opposite sex, rather than a therapist of the same sex, in order to facilitate the first stage of counseling, since both male and female clients seem to prefer an attractive therapist. Over and above the attractiveness dimension, it appears that clients are slightly less critical of a therapist of the opposite sex.

Attractiveness and the Counseling Process

The data presented here lends support to Strong's (1968) contention that counseling for attitudinal and behavioral changes is a two-phase process. The bulk of the data suggest that the client's perception of therapist attributes such as expertness, trustworthiness, and general skillfulness is enhanced by physical attractiveness. According to Strong, the client's perceptions of these attributes should increase the ability of the therapist to influence the client in counseling by increasing the client's involvement. In the Vargas and Borkowski studies (1982, 1983), for example, the dependent measure was future expectations, reflecting level of involvement in, and commitment to, therapy. Attractive therapists receive greater commitment from clients to future therapy. These findings support Strong's notions about Stage 1 and Stage 2 in the counseling process.

The research reviewed in this chapter may be disconcerting to those counselors and clinicians who believe that physical attributes, such as physical attractiveness, do not have an effect on the therapeutic process. It is "normal" that most therapists would like to believe that physical attractiveness does not enter as an essential factor in determining the success of therapy. Most would be more content to hold that interpersonal factors such as skillfulness, integrity, and caring are essential attributes in influencing therapeutic change. In spite of our most cherished beliefs, however, it cannot be overlooked that the research cited in this chapter challenges prevalent ways of thinking about the determinants of therapeutic outcomes. Although a therapist's actual skills, in combination with positive personality characteristics, are extremely important, it appears that physical attractiveness is also a major variable in Stage 1 processes and perhaps in eventual Stage 2 outcomes. It is possible that many people would not continue past the initial stage of therapy if they were being counseled by an unattractive therapist, unless that person were highly skilled, insightful, and flexible.

What is the relevance for therapy of the data cited here? One implication seems to be that therapists need to consider, rather than dismiss outright, physical attractiveness as a component in the therapeutic process. Of course, we do not advocate screening applicants prior to admission to graduate school in terms of GRE scores, grades, personal skills, *and attractiveness*. Rather, we think it feasible to focus on the importance of personal appearance in training counselors. It should be emphasized that our actresses played both roles — unattractive and attractive counselors. And it was their personal presentation — or secondary features of attractiveness — that differentiated actresses in their dual roles. Our data suggested that clothing, cosmetics, fitness, and grooming determine perceptions about physical attractiveness. Thus, we argue that novice counselors need to respect the role played by "appearance" in leading to more substantial aspects of Stage 1 processes, such as their client's judgments about sincerity and trustworthiness.

Research Directions

Apparently, Strong (1968) orginally intended his two-phase model to apply regardless of the therapist's particular orientation. More specifically, he proposed that in Stage 2 the therapist uses the influence base established in Stage 1 to effect desired changes through a wide variety of techniques. "The exact techniques he (therapist) uses will depend on his diagnosis of the problem, the facilities available, his own expertise, and his guiding theoretical model. He may use interpretation, suggestion, advice, urging, information, homework assignments, reinforcement, role playing, modeling, behavioral enactment and practice, and other techniques" (p. 223). This claim suggests a new direction for future research: Does physical attractiveness have the same implications for therapeutic orientations other than the non-directive (cf. Rogers, 1957)? It is important to assess the effects of physical attractiveness on therapeutic outcomes when embedded in more directive therapies or in behavior-modification procedures.

Additional research on the influence of physical attractiveness on both the first and second stages of counseling is needed to lend support to the implications drawn here. Research needs to address the relative importance of physical attractiveness in relation to therapist attributes that are more subject to alteration and enhancement. The study by Vargas and Borkowski (1982) indicated that attractiveness interacts with skillfulness in certain situations. We suspect that various combinations of skills, therapeutic approaches, and counselor styles will override the attractiveness effect or diminish its impact during the initial phases of therapy.

There is no doubt that counseling is indeed a more complex process than once theorized (Mitchell, Bozarth, & Krauft, 1977; Vargas and Borkowski, 1983). It is the unraveling of this complexity, such as the casual influence of attractiveness judgments on subsequent perceptions about expertness and trustworthiness in the context of various counseling methods, that requires our future theoretical and research attention.

CHAPTER 10

THE STAGES OF INFLUENCE IN COUNSELING AND PSYCHOTHERAPY

TERENCE J. TRACEY

VIEWING COUNSELING and psychotherapy as influence processes is becoming much more common, as is evidenced by this volume and recent research in the area. Much of the research has focused on how the counselor influences the client. The assumption being that if we know how the counselor influences the client, then we can influence our clients more effectively. However, this approach neglects the effect or influence the client has on the counselor. Although much recognition is given to the concept of mutual influence, little research and conceptualization has been done from this perspective. If the concept of mutual influence is valid, then it would be expected that the influence attempts of each of the participants would vary over time, reflecting the cumulative effect that each person had on the other. In this view, the influence of either participant is not a static trait. Examination of the influence process thus requires a study of how each person attempts to influence the other over time. The purpose of this chapter is to present a stage model of successful counseling/psychotherapy that focuses on how the client and counselor attempt to influence each other over the course of treatment.

The goal of treatment in this model is to enable the client to be effective in his or her influence attempts. It is assumed that all individuals attempt to influence their environment, i.e. other people, to meet their needs. Clients seek help because they are not as successful as they would like to be in getting their needs met. The task of the counselor is to help the client gain more appropriate means of influencing others to better meet his or her needs. The manner of achieving this task requires that the counselor first recognize how the client attempts to influence his or her environment and then work to get the client to try new means of influence that would be more realistic and effective. The accomplishment of this change in client influence attempts is hypothesized to be associated with three relatively distinct stages of the counseling interaction. Each stage represents a different influence strategy that the counselor uses in response to client influence attempts. It is proposed that all three stages are necessary for successful outcome. Partial movement through the three stages is associated with less successful outcome.

Early Stage

The first stage relates to establishing rapport with the client, which implies that the goal of this stage is for the client to feel understood and valued. The attainment of rapport is proposed to be a function of the extent to which the counselor acts in a manner in line with the client's influence attempts. All clients enter counseling with certain expectations regarding what is to occur, e.g. what each person is to do, what are appropriate foci, and how topics should be discussed. These expectations are both conscious and unconscious, and the client attempts to influence the counselor into acting according to them in both explicit and subtle ways. Implied in these expectations are certain preferred behaviors from the counselor which the client attempts to elicit (Beier, 1966; Kell & Mueller, 1966). If the counselor behaves according to these expectations, the client should feel understood and valued, because the counselor is following the client's definition of what should occur. The less the counselor adheres to the client's expectations and influence attempts, the less the client will feel understood and valued. Successful traversing of this initial stage of rapport attainment is dependent upon the counselor (1) accurately perceiving the relationship expectations of the client, both realistic and unrealistic, and (2) acting according to them.

An example of poor negotiation of the rapport stage would be the client who enters counseling strongly expressing a desire to keep things on an intellectual level, yet who is also expressing, albeit much less clearly, particular areas of pain and a desire for comfort. The client will be attempting to get the counselor to act both on an overt intellectual and a covert emotional level. The extent to which the counselor can act according to both, somewhat conflicting and unrealistic client influence attempts, will be the extent to which the client will feel understood. If the counselor responds to only one of the influence attempts (e.g. overt discussion of pain), the client will not feel completely understood.

If the counselor does not do an adequate job of recognizing and meeting client expectations, it could be expected that the client would terminate prematurely (Lennard & Bernstein, 1967), as his or her needs were not met. Thus, successful movement through this early, rapport stage is a function of the extent to which the counselor is able to accept the client's "neurotic" relationship definition and influence attempts.

Middle Stage

If the initial rapport building stage has been successfully managed, what exists is a relationship determined relatively exclusively by the client. By accepting the client's definition of the relationship, the counselor has reinforced the client's unrealistic definition of the relationship. It is assumed that these unrealistic, "neurotic" relationship expectations and associated relationship influence attempts are the client's problem. The client has defined the relationship in a manner that reduces client anxiety by not allowing the counselor to have any input. The middle stage is characterized by the counselor changing tactics and not acting so much according to client relationship definition.

This alteration of counselor behavior results in a conflict over who is to influence what will occur. Each participant is trying to define the relationship and influence the other based on his or her own definitions while not accepting the definitions of the other. As the counselor starts to try and relate to the client in more realistic ways, e.g. by being more direct about some of the earlier implicit messages, the client becomes more anxious and feels less understood. The client wishes to return to the old, comfortable relationship and attempts to influence the counselor to act accordingly. To influence the counselor to go back to earlier ways of acting, the client will resort to very powerful and unrealistic influence ploys; an extreme example of which would be to threaten suicide. The counselor in this middle stage should resist acting completely according to client unrealistic expectations and influence attempts. What results is each person resisting, to some extent, what the other wants. The client desires a reestablishment of the initial unrealistic, "neurotic" relationship, where he or she felt very comfortable, and the counselor is attempting to get the client to relate in a realistic, give-and-take, mutually determined manner.

It is this conflict stage that results in change in the client. The more the counselor does not act according to the client's definition, the more the client will increase his or her influence attempts to bring the relationship back to where it was. The counselor will resist these influence attempts. This continued counselor resistance to the client's attempts to return the relationship to the earlier position will stimulate client change. With time, the client will be forced to start adopting more realistic views of the relationship, or at least be more open to mutual definition. This openness to mutual relationship definition is indicative of more healthy functioning. This change process can be explained by viewing the counselor's behavior as not reinforcing the client's unrealistic influence attempts. Given this lack of reinforcement and a probable prior history of intermittent reinforcement, it would be expected that the client would increase unrealistic influence attempts to obtain reinforcement. Then, as little further reinforcement would be forthcoming, the client would start using new behaviors that would be more likely to be reinforced by others (Beier, 1966).

Successful movement through this middle, conflict stage is dependent upon the counselor skillfully maintaining a balance between conforming to (support) and acting different from (conflict) client unrealistic expectations. If the counselor acts according to the client's definition, i.e. the counselor introduces little new behavior, the relationship will be viewed by both participants as fairly comfortable. No change will occur. Conversely, too much conflict, caused by the counselor acting very differently from the initial agreed relationship definition, can result in premature termination. It is assumed that what keeps the client in treatment is the hope of returning to the earlier, comfortable relationship where one's needs were met, albeit unrealistically. If the current counseling relationship is too discrepant from the earlier one, it would be harder for clients to sustain this hope and easier just to give up by withdrawing. The amount of conflict introduced by the counselor in this middle stage must be constantly monitored.

This optimal amount of conflict and its timing (abruptness vs. gradualness) is hypothesized to be related to the disturbance level of the client. The healthy client can endure more conflict and, as such, much more therapist deviation from expectation is possible. Movement into the middle, conflict stage could thus be much more abrupt, given the client's resources. However, more disturbed clients would require much more support and could endure much less conflict. Movement into the middle stage would have to be slow and gradual, with the counselor deviating only slightly from the original expectations. Thus, treatment would be much longer. For the more disturbed client, too high a conflict/support ratio can result in withdrawal (either physically or psychologically), while the exact same conflict/support ratio may not be enough to affect change in a healthier client. So, successful travel through this middle conflict stage requires the counselor to be able to: (a) assess the optimal conflict/support level that can be used to effect client change, and (b) be flexible enough to vary his or her behavior away from initially agreed behaviors to achieve this optimum balance.

Late Stage

The final-resolution stage comes about as the client starts to develop more realistic relationship definitions. The client becomes less wedded to unrealistic, unilateral definitions of what is to occur in the relationship. He or she begins to notice the counselor as a real person, with his or her own input, for the first time. How each person is to act with the other is openly negotiated for the first time. The initial counseling relationship was based exclusively on the client's definitions. As clients treat the therapeutic relationship more realistically, they are also approaching outside issues, problems, and relationships equally realistically. Again, there is harmony in the relationship, but, instead of being based exclusively on the client's definition as in the initial stage, it is based on a mutual definition of what is to occur. In this stage, the client experiments with a variety of new behaviors and relationship definitions to get a feel for his or her level of comfort. This is often an exciting yet threatening stage, but the client is dealing with the anxiety openly and is largely amenable to feedback, unlike previously. In this stage, the counselor is more free to act as a real person and to give opinions. But often-times, this is when the counselor is least required, as the client is better able to openly address his or her needs in ways that others, outside treatment, can respond. Much of the reinforcement of new appropriate behavior should occur outside of counseling.

Overall, a three-stage model has been proposed and defined by three different tasks of the counselor. The counselor first behaves in accordance with client influence attempts and relationship definition (rapport stage), then the counselor alters his or her behavior away from the client definition (conflict stage), and, finally, as the client is able to deal realistically with the relationship, the counselor pulls back and initiates termination. The central dimension of this stage model is its focus on the communication between the participants as the vehicle of influence. Specifically, the proposed model is reflected in the relative communicational harmony between the participants. The first and third stages are hypothesized to have relatively harmonious communication, because each participant's actions are understood and agreed upon by the other, even though the initial relationship is client determined and the later relationship is more mutually determined. The middle stage, on the other hand, should demonstrate somewhat less harmonious communication (less agreements, less following of other's topics or desires, more conflict, and more open expression of negative affect) because what each person should do is much less in agreement. With respect to communicational harmony, then, the proposed stage model will evidence a high-low-high pattern over time.

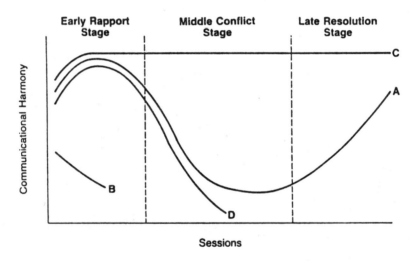

Figure 10-1. Graphs of the hypothesized pattern of communicational harmony over the course of treatment. Line A represents successful counseling. Lines B through D represent the three types of unsuccessful outcome associated with this model. Line B represents a failure to achieve rapport. Line C represents a failure to enter the conflict stage. Line D represents the introduction of too much conflict.

A graph of this proposed model of successful counseling is presented as line A in Figure 10-1. The other lines in Figure 10-1 depict the various ways that counseling could result in a less successful outcome. Line B represents a failure to establish rapport due to the counselor not acting according to client expectations and influence attempts. The client will try harder to get the counselor to understand and to act accordingly, while the counselor will be trying harder to define what is to occur in his or her own way. Communication will not be harmonious, as neither will be acting as the other desires. If continued over time, each will become dissatisfied and most likely the client will fail to return. Line C represents a failure on the counselor's part to move the relationship into the middle conflict stage. The counselor continues to act according to the early client definitions of the relationship and thus each other's actions are not in conflict. No change is introduced in the counselor's behavior, and thus no client change will result. Line D represents what occurs if the counselor introduces too much change in behavior during the middle conflict stage. This large change in counselor behavior results in an increase in communicational conflict, but the amount of conflict is too much for the client to endure. The promise of returning to the more harmonious early stage appears impossible given the current disharmony, so the client terminates.

The validity of the proposed stage model has been examined in only a few studies. Dietzel and Abeles (1975) and Tracey and Ray (1984) have found support for the hypothesized high-low-high pattern of communicational harmony in successful counseling, and the flat profile (line C) for the unsuccessful work. Duehn and Proctor (1977) found support for the presence of line B of Figure 10-1. Communicational disharmony (assessed by the extent to which the participants could agree on topics of conversation) was found to be higher in those dyads that terminated prematurely. Overall, there is some support for the validity of the proposed stage model, although much more work is needed. But, the hypothesized model also has some interesting implications regarding client-counselor matching.

Client-Counselor Matching

Given the importance of the counselor acting according to the client's relationship definition in the early stage, it makes sense to assign clients to counselors who would be more likely to match their expectations. For example, counselors vary greatly on the extent to which they are able or desire to structure the interaction. Those clients who expect a directive counselor would probably feel more comfortable and understood with a counselor who manifested these directive and structuring behaviors. In principle, matching clients with counselors who have a greater likelihood of behaving according to client expectations would lead to quicker rapport and fewer premature terminations.

The key to client assignment would thus be the relative similarity of client expectations to the behavior repertoire of the counselor. If this discrepancy were great, it would be presumed to be more difficult to establish rapport. Conversely, given great similarity of client expectations and counselor behavior, it would be very easy to establish a quick and strong rapport. But the research examining this hypothesis has yielded equivocal results (Duckro, Beal, & George, 1979).

There are three major problems with the matching concept. The first and most glaring is measurement of client expectations, especially some of the unrealistic and covertly expressed ones. With more disturbed clients, this assessment would be especially difficult because a greater proportion would be covert and conflicting. Given the subtle nature of these expectations it is hard to assume that paper-and-pencil measures would be able to reflect the entire domain, although this may be a start. Perhaps the best means of assessing these dimensions appears to be an assessment of the client by a particularly skilled counselor(s) who would be sensitive to these subtle role expectations. This type of diagnostic assessment is what has been called for by McLemore and Benjamin (1979).

Even given excellent measurement of the client's role expectations, the issue of counselor skill is paramount. Some counselors are flexible enough in behavior that, although they may prefer one type of behavior in counseling, they are able to adapt to a wide variety of client expectations. Other counselors are skilled in establishing rapport with only those clients whose expectations fit the style they prefer. It seems plausible to propose that client-counselor matching will yield three distinct groupings: (1) those with an excellent match which will almost certainly result in a well-established rapport, (2) those with a moderate mismatch of client expectations with counselor preferred behavior which would result in unclear rapport, and (3) those of great mismatch where it would be almost impossible to establish rapport. It seems obvious that if the client's expectations match well with the counselor's preferred behavior, that rapport would come easy. Similarly, if the client expected the counselor to act in a manner extremely different from the counselor's preference and ability, it would be extremely difficult to establish rapport. The grouping where counselor skill is expected to make the most impact is the middle group of moderate discrepancy. Skilled counselors would be those who could adapt their behavior somewhat to meet the expectations of the client. Less skilled counselors would be those who would have more trouble altering their behavior or style. Although all counselors could be very effective in helping their clients, as defined here a skilled counselor would be one who is more flexible in counseling style and thus would be able to establish rapport with a greater range of clients.

The other drawback to matching is that even if the client and counselor were perfectly matched, there is no guarantee that the matched dyads would result in better outcome. Matching is only hypothesized to be related to attainment of initial rapport, not movement through the conflict or resolution stages. In fact, it may be expected that a perfect match of client expectations and counselor-preferred behavior may be detrimental to a successful outcome. Given a good match, it may be harder for the counselor to alter his or her behavior in the middle stage so as to stimulate client change. If the counselor is quite comfortable in the initial role, it would be presumably more difficult for him or her to change behavior, as changing would feel inappropriate to the counselor. A common example of this is the counselor's encouragement of client dependence in the middle stages rather than the counselor attempting to stimulate independence.

Conclusions and Implications

The model proposed here involves viewing counseling and psychotherapy as a process whereby each participant is attempting to influence the other. Successful outcome is proposed to be a function of the counselor skillfully adopting three relatively separate influence strategies over the course of treatment. Poor use of counselor influence is proposed to be related to less or unsuccessful outcome. The proposed model has implications for practice, research, and training.

The stage model presents the counselor with a relatively easily monitored means of assessing one's progress in treatment. If the counselor realizes that rapport is hard to establish, he or she may start looking for the subtle and conflicting expectations and influence attempts that had been overlooked. Similarly, if the counselor notices that the dyad has not moved into the conflict stage, he or she would start to look for ways that this could be accomplished. Obviously, more validation of the model is required, but it does provide some cues as to altering counselor behavior to effect change.

The proposed stage model implies that reseachers should look for differences in client and therapist influence over the entire course of treatment. If the model is valid, studies that examine only a few sessions of actual counseling or psychotherapy would yield only very partial results which could not at all be said to be representative of what occurs in treatment. Also, given the great variability in rates of movement through the different stages, it makes little sense to aggregate process data across dyads by session numbers. One dyad could be engaged in the conflict stage in session two while another dyad is just starting to establish rapport. Aggregating these two dyads to represent early counseling would not be valid in either case.

Finally, as depicted in this model, the successful counselor is required to have three skills: (a) the ability to recognize the realistic and unrealistic expectations of the client, be they clearly or implicitly expressed, (b) an ability to alter his or her own behavior to meet these client expectations, and (c) an ability to know the right amount of behavior change to introduce for stimulating change, yet not overwhelming the client. These skills require counselor perceptiveness (to recognize subtle and conflicting client expectations) and flexibility (to change behavior according need). In this model the counselor is expected to engage in three separate types of influence behaviors at different points in the treatment process. Counselors with very strong behavior preferences or with a restricted behavioral repertoire will be at a disadvantage, as they will only be able to treat successfully a smaller range of clients and/or they will have difficulty in making the transitions between stages. An ability to act in a variety of ways in response to any stimulus is key to skillful practice, and we should make attempts to expand our trainee's behavioral repertoire.

CHAPTER 11

A SOCIAL INFLUENCE INTERPRETATION
OF THE ADLERIAN VOCATIONAL
COUNSELING PROCESS

C. EDWARD WATKINS, JR.

ADLERIAN VOCATIONAL theory is an extension of Alfred
Adler's (1956) theoretical formulations to the vocational domain.
Adlerian vocational theory (Watkins, 1984a) is a social psychological approach to understanding vocational development; it shares much in
common with social influence theory. This chapter considers briefly
some of the ways in which Adlerian vocational theory practically relates
to social influence theory.

The Concept of Life Style

In Adlerian vocational theory, each individual is considered to
possess three life attitudes: (a) attitude toward self, (b) attitude toward
others, and (c) attitude toward the world in general. The self-attitude
consists of thoughts, feelings, and views about oneself. The "other" attitude consists of thoughts, feelings, and views about others. The attitude
toward the world consists of views that individuals hold about the world
(for example, is the world a fair, unfair, or neutral place?). These three
attitudes significantly influence individuals' thoughts about vocational
development, the place of work as a life task, and the type of work in
which they wish to engage. In vocational counseling, these attitudes
need to be given attention and examined for the important vocational
data that they can provide. From both an Adlerian and social influence

perspective, the attitudes about self, others, and the world are social attitudes that are integral to the vocational counseling process.

The life attitudes collectively are called the *life style*. The life style is the characteristic manner in which individuals perceive, think about, respond to and act on the world about them. The life style is the general frame of reference that brings order and organization to the world. To assist individuals who come for vocational counseling, the counselor's knowledge about and understanding of each client's life style is important. To develop life style understanding, the counselor strives to engage clients in the vocational counseling process. The vocational counseling process consists of four stages: (a) establishing the counselor-client relationship, (b) psychological investigation, (c) interpretation, and (d) reorientation. These four stages will be described and their social influence bases will be presented.

An Adlerian Approach to Vocational Counseling

The Counselor-Client Relationship

In Adlerian vocational counseling, the first step is to establish a therapeutic relationship with the client. The counselor strives to build rapport and develop a relationship bond with the client. During this stage, the counselor attempts to listen effectively to the client and facilitate the client's self-exploration. The counselor's implementation of empathy, respect and warmth, and other core conditions (Rogers, 1957) is critical. The primary task of the counselor is to assist the client in expressing himself or herself. As a corollary task, the counselor strives not to exhibit any behaviors that would impede or restrict the client's self-expression.

In conjunction with verbal behaviors, counselor nonverbal behaviors are also considerably important (Dinkmeyer, Pew, & Dinkmeyer, 1979). The counselor strives to nonverbally communicate attentiveness to and interest in the client. Important counselor behaviors include maintaining good eye contact, facing the client physically, and being physically receptive (open body posture) to the client. Nonverbally, the counselor wants to communicate that "I am with you."

During this initial stage, the Adlerian vocational counselor builds on three social influence power bases: expertness, attractiveness, and trustworthiness. As for expertness, the Adlerian model draws on verbal and nonverbal behaviors that contribute to the counselor's expert status, for example, attentiveness, interest in the client, the core conditions, direct eye contact, appropriate trunk posture, head nodding, and sense of confidence (Schmidt & Strong, 1970). To enhance attractiveness, the counselor engages in effective listening behaviors and responds only as needed (Kleinke & Tully, 1979). In responding, Adlerians use a variety of response modes (Dinkmeyer et al., 1979); empathy and self-disclosure are two response modes that Adlerians use to enhance their attractiveness (see Merluzzi, Banikiotes, & Missbach, 1978). In enhancing trustworthiness, many of the previous verbal and nonverbal behaviors are drawn on (Kaul & Schmidt, 1971; Merluzzi et al., 1978). To establish an effective counselor-client relationship, the Adlerian counselor attempts to establish a power base through enhancing expertness, attractiveness, and trustworthiness.

Psychological Investigation

During the second stage of Adlerian vocational counseling, the counselor attempts to develop an understanding of the client's life style. To understand the life style, the counselor engages in a psychological investigation that is designed to provide such information. In conducting the investigation, the counselor asks the client about his or her: (a) views about self, others, and life; (b) approach to the life tasks of work and social relationships; (c) descriptions of and perceptions about relationships with father, mother and siblings; and (d) early recollections, among other areas (see Adler, 1956; Watkins, 1982). All of this information enables the counselor to gain insight into the client's individualized way of approaching life. Through understanding the life style, the counselor can develop hypotheses about such areas as the client's manner of interacting with co-workers, vocational interests, and occupational satisfaction (Watkins, 1984a).

In conjuction with the life style investigation, the counselor can also use interest inventories and ability measures. For example, the *Self-Directed Search* (Holland, 1979a) is a useful tool for identifying life style preferences. The six Holland personality types (Holland, 1973) — realistic, investigative, artistic, social, enterprising, and conventional — are each life styles; they provide life style information that can be integral to the Adlerian vocational counseling process. Therefore, the counselor can use both life style interviews and life style inventories for vocational assessment purposes.

While the social power bases of attractiveness and trustworthiness remain important, the counselor as psychological investigator primarily draws on the expertness and informational power bases. From an informational perspective, the counselor explains: (a) the purposes of the life style interview and testing procedures; (b) what is involved in the interview and testing procedures (for example, how they proceed, what they require of the client, how long they take to complete); and (c) what the client can hope to gain from them. Such information contributes to the client's understanding, involves the client in the counseling process, and informs the client that the counselor is fully aware of the assessments' purposes and their outcome. From the perspective of expertness, the interview and testing procedures contribute to the client's image of the counselor as an expert. The counselor is seen as someone who knows about personality and interest assessment and is able to use his or her knowledge to help others. Thus, the counselor as expert possesses an important body of knowledge that can assist the client, but it is a body of knowledge of which the client is unaware and one that he or she needs.

Interpretation

During the interpretation stage of Adlerian vocational counseling, the counselor interprets the life style interview and testing information to the client. The meaning of the data is communicated to the client, and the implications of the data are presented. The manner in which the interpretation stage is approached will vary from counselor to counselor. Some counselors view their role to be one of imparting interpretive information to a client who is unaware. Other counselors view the interpretive stage as a collaborative effort between themselves and their clients; they ask clients about their interpretations of the data and what it means to them (for example, see Watkins, 1984b). Whatever the approach taken, the counselor's goal is to clearly and concisely provide the client with information about his or her personality characteristics, abilities and vocational interests. This information, it is hoped, will assist the client to more meaningfully explore and consider vocational possibilities.

The expertness power base is important in the interpretation stage. As an expert, the counselor is someone who possesses the knowledge and expertise to gather relevant information, analyze it, and offer interpretive statements or conclusions to the client. In other words, the counselor, whose knowledge and expertise derive from his or her professional training and experience, is someone who knows the meaning of the data. In sharing the meaning of the data, the informational power base again becomes important. Two factors primarily contribute to the counselor's informational power: (a) assessment sources (life style interview, interest inventories, ability measures) and (b) the counselor's presentation of the information. During the interpretation stage, the counselor presents the assessment data to the client, explains the meaning of the data, and indicates the possible implications of the data for the client. A clear and concise communication of the data can also contribute to the counselor's informational power. The counselor is seen as someone who possesses important information that the client needs. All of these factors work together in allowing the counselor to build and draw on an informational power base.

Reorientation

Once some understanding about personality characteristics, abilities, and vocational interests has been gained, the client often is able to examine vocational possibilities more decisively. He or she has some valuable information that can be of help in narrowing the vocational search, suggesting possible career directions, and suggesting more limited vocational areas that merit further exploration. The counselor functions in a facilitative capacity, helping the client to consider career options and positive and negative aspects about them. The counselor also instructs the client about important informational sources (for example, *Occupational Outlook Handbook, Dictionary of Occupational Titles*) that can be of help in gaining more specific and detailed career information. Other strategies, such as suggesting that the client take a certain part-time job to test out career interests or interview individuals working in certain vocations, can be used, depending on the client's needs and level of decisiveness. The purposes of the reorientation stage are twofold: (a) to assist the client in continuing to actively participate in the career-decision process, and (b) to provide the client with information, sources, and other aids that will facilitate the process.

The informational and ecological power bases are particularly important during the reorientation stage. From an informational perspective, the counselor, an expert who knows about sources of occupational information, must effectively inform the client about these sources. For example, in telling a client about the *Occupational Outlook Handbook,* the counselor needs to: (a) explain the purposes of the handbook, (b) explain how it can be of value to the client, (c) explain the format of the handbook, and (d) illustrate how to use it. Two aspects contribute to the counselor's informational power base: (a) the counselor's knowledge about the existence of the informational source, and (b) the counselor's knowledge on how to effectively use the source.

Ecologically, the counselor knows about actions or environmental opportunities that can facilitate the client's career-exploration process. The counselor's knowledge about environmental manipulations and communication of these to the client contribute to an ecological power base. For instance, a simple suggestion that empowers the client to act on his or her environment can be helpful (e.g. "After individuals identify occupations that are of interest to them, they often find it valuable to interview people who work in those occupations. I would suggest that you consider interviewing people employed in the occupations that are of interest to you. I have a card file here with names of individuals who would be willing to tell you about their work."). Similar suggestions and recommendations further enhance the ecological power base that exists in the counseling relationship. More importantly, such suggestions can also assist the client to make a more informed career decision.

Conclusion

Social influence theory is a meta-model that is applicable to both the personal and vocational counseling relationships. This chapter has considered briefly some ways in which social influence theory is applicable to a specific vocational counseling approach: Adlerian vocational counseling. The power bases of expertness, attractiveness, and trustworthiness seem to be important throughout the four stages of the Adlerian vocational counseling process. As the process proceeds, the informational and ecological power bases become increasingly important. Although Adlerian vocational theory and its counseling applications are rudimentary in their development, the social influence model appears helpful in conceptualizing the roles and functions of the Adlerian vocational counselor.

CHAPTER 12

METHODOLOGICAL APPROACHES TO THE STUDY OF INTERPERSONAL INFLUENCE IN COUNSELING INTERACTION

JAMES W. LICHTENBERG
AND EDWARD J. HECK

THE ISSUE OF social interaction, irrespective of subjects or context, rests fundamentally on an assumption of behavioral dependency between participants. Persons are said to be "interacting" (in contrast to simply behaving) whenever they respond in a non-random or contingent manner with respect to each other. Although the degree of contingency among persons' responses may vary depending on the persons and the context, to the extent that contingency exists between the responses of interactants, it may be said that the interactants influence the responses of each other.

The assumption of interdependency is valid for counseling and psychotherapy. Indeed, were counselors and clients not to respond to each other in an contingent manner, it would be difficult to say that counseling transpired. Clients come to counselors for help and ask to be influenced, and counselors seek to influence their clients by their helping behaviors. At the same time, clients influence the ways in which their counselors give that help.

Social influence has generally been construed in one of three ways: (a) in terms of the person's power bases or potential to influence, (b) in terms of the nature of the interaction process through which influence is exerted, and (c) in terms of outcomes or consequences (Olson & Cromwell, 1975). Within the context of counseling and psychotherapy, most of the theorizing and research regarding social influence has focused on power bases — particularly those of the counselor (e.g. Strong, 1968; Strong & Matross, 1973; see review of this research by Corrigan et al., 1980) and power outcomes (Carson, 1969; also see Anchin, 1982). To date there appears to be little work, either theoretical or empirical, on the social influence within counseling from a *process* perspective. It is with respect to this perspective that we wish to focus this chapter. In particular, our intent in this chapter is to present some of our thinking on the social interaction and social influence processes that occur within counseling and psychotherapy and several research methods and strategies that hold promise for illuminating those processes.

The Character of Social Interaction

Characteristic of social interaction in general, and of counseling and psychotherapy in particular, are three basic features: sequentiality, flexibility and constraint (Raush, 1965).

SEQUENTIALITY. Within counseling the individual responses of counselors and clients, their interactive behaviors, as well as the interviews they comprise, are temporally organized and sequentially ordered. Counseling outcomes do not emerge full-blown, rather they evolve sequentially having reference to previous and future steps in the counseling process. Irrespective of the units of the counseling process that we choose to observe, whether individual behaviors or complete interviews, the process does not run backwards.

FLEXIBILITY. While one might wish to argue a case for determinism, social interaction data appear to obey probabilistic rules rather than strictly deterministic laws. Probabilism means that although the effect of counselor and client responses on the other may be reasonably predictable, some degree of randomness or flexibility exists within their interaction.

CONSTRAINT. Despite its randomness or flexibility, counseling is generally not chaotic. Out of all the possible response variability that potentially may occur, some semblance of order generally emerges in the interaction. This occurs because the interactive responses are not completely random but are contingent upon, or to some degree constrained by, each other's responses. What counselors do and say is presumed to be some reasonable function of what their clients do and say, and counselors' responses are presumed to have some impact upon their clients' responses.

This constraint within the counseling interaction may be either direct or indirect. The constraint or influence of a response is *direct* when the impact is immediate; it is *indirect* or remote when the impact is mediated by intervening responses.

Patterns of Constraint and Influence in Counseling Interaction

As social interaction, the process of counseling consists of a series of behavior exchanges between a counselor and a client. This series of exchanges may be understood to be a probabilistic or stochastic process (Lichtenberg & Hummel, 1976) over which the response variability of *both* the client and the counselor undergo modification and constraint. In this regard, the process of counseling can be viewed as a process of mutual and reciprocal social influence.

Regardless of how one chooses to characterize or categorize the individual responses of a counselor and client during their interaction, the process of counseling may be viewed as a series of transitions from counselor response to client response to counselor response, and so on. Each transition represents a particular response-response contingency within the process, and the analysis of their interaction may consist of an analysis of those contingencies.

A fundamental assumption underlying this view of counseling is that the behavior of each participant at any point in time in the process is, at least to some degree, contingent upon (i.e. influenced by) past acts within the interaction. For example, counselors' questions are generally followed by client answers, and clients' answers (whatever they might be) are likely to be pursued by the counselor in terms of that response. Such a pattern of responding, one in which a response by either the counselor or client is contingent upon the immediately preceding response of the other, exemplifies direct influence and defines what is generally referred to as a "first-order process" (i.e. a process that evidences first-order dependency among its events).

It is possible that the responses of counselors and clients within the counseling process are of an order of dependency greater than one and that the influence or constraint among events within the process is indirect or remote. For example, a person's responses at some time t may be dependent not only upon the other person's immediately preceding response (at time $t - 1$) but also upon the person's own previous response (at time $t - 2$). The counseling interaction in this instance would be said to evidence second-order dependency.

Were the interactants' responses within counseling to be contingent upon the preceding three responses (e.g. the client's response at time t

being dependent on the counselor's response at time $t - 1$, the client's own previous response at time $t - 2$, and the counselor's response at time $t - 3$), the interaction would be said to evidence third-order dependency.

It is possible, of course, for clients' responses to be virtually uninfluenced by those of their counselor but nevertheless evidence constraint, and the same may be true for the counselor. In such instances, the speakers influence their own responding but not that of the other. This pattern of constraint may be first order or greater and is referred to as "self-contingent" responding. Although it would not constitute "social influence" in the sense that we mean it in this chapter, it nevertheless is a possible pattern of influence.

Finally, the possibility of an absence of any dependency (zero-order dependency) among counselor and client responses within the counseling process should be acknowledged. In such a case, neither the counselor's nor the client's responses would be constrained by the other or by themselves. Not only would there be an absence of "interaction" and dialogue between the counselor and the client, but there would also be an absence of coherence or monologue on either person's part.

Analyzing the Influence Process: A General Example

Suppose that one observes a sequence of counselor-client exhanges using two observational codes (A and B). If one were to observe the interaction sequence ABAABABBABBAAABABBABAAABBAAABB, one could describe the interaction sequence by simply observing that the frequency of occurrence of A is 16, and that the frequency of B is 14. Within the sequence there were a total of 30 distinct responses. The unconditional probability (simple likelihood of occurrence) of an A response within that interaction sequence is thus $p(A) = 16/30 = .53$; and the unconditional probability of a B response within the sequence is $p(B) = 14/30 = .47$. From this perspective, the likelihood of an A response is greater than that of a B response.

One may, however, analyze the interaction sequence in terms of the contingencies between A and B responses. The probability of occurrence of A, given that it is immediately preceded by B, is the conditional (contingent) probability of A given B or $p(A|B)$. Response B occurs as an antecedent response in a contingency 13 times in the sequence (the final B response in the interaction sequence does not serve as an antecedent). Of those 13 occurrences, A occurs immediately after B eight times. Thus, the proportion of times that the occurrence of B is followed by A (or the proportion of times that A is preceded by B) is 8/13, and the conditional probability $p(A|B) = .62$. The probability of occurrence of A, given that it is immediately preceded by (i.e. contingent on) its own prior occurrence, is the proportion of times A occurs after an A response. An A response occurs as an antecedent response 16 times and it is followed by another A response 7 times. Thus, $p(A|A) = 7/16 = .44$. The probability of occurrence of B, given that it is preceded by A, is $p(B|A) = 9/16 = .56$; and the conditional probability of B, given an immediately preceding occurrence of B, is $p(B|B) = 5/13 = .38$.

It should be clear from the above example that knowledge of the immediately preceding event in the interaction sequence may alter one's predictions concerning the "next event." In this case, knowing that B occurred at time $t - 1$ would lead to increased certainty that the next response in the interaction would be an A and not a B.

To the degree that the responses within a social interaction sequence "depend on" or are contingent upon preceding responses, those responses may be said to be influenced by the preceding responses. That influence may act to "inhibit" the occurrence of a particular response or class of responses, or it may act to "excite" or increase the likelihood of certain responses.

In the example just given, only the effects of the immediately preceding response on the subsequent response were presented. In the several methods to be presented below, the dependency among responses need not be limited to the influence effect of immediately preceding events; rather, each allows for the investigation of more complex and distal/remote patterns of influence.

Markov Models

One of the simplest statistical approaches to studying patterns of influence in counseling is the Markov chain model. There are two assumptions that are central to such models. The first assumption is that the current response in the interaction, irrespective of the person making that response, is contingent upon recent past responses. The second assumption is that the degree of contingency between the previous response(s) and the current response is stable (or stationary) across time (Chatfield, 1973).

Using the example of a "counselor-client interaction sequence" that was presented earlier, it is possible to describe the sequence of coded responses in the sequence by specifying the likelihood of the various possible response-response contingencies or response "transitions." This is essentially what was done earlier when the first-order conditional probabilities were determined for the sequence. These transition probabilities can then be arranged in a matrix called a *transition matrix* in which the rows of the matrix represent each of the possible contingency antecedent events and the matrix columns represent each of the possible contingency consequents. Such a matrix thus summarizes the probabilities of each possible response in the sequence following every other response at the next (t) instance.

To the extent that the probabilities within and across each row are not equal, the antecedent responses may be said to constrain or modify the distribution of the probabilities of the various consequents. If the occurrence of a response is constrained by only the immediately preceding response, and if the probabilities are stationary across the sequence, the sequence is said to exhibit first-order dependency and constitute a first-order Markov chain.

As already noted, it is possible that the interaction between counselors and clients would show a higher order of dependency among responses. For example, a counselor's interpretative comment to a client more than likely is dependent on a number of different client responses that the client has made rather than just the immediately preceding one.

To investigate the possibility of higher orders of dependency among events, one constructs higher-order contingency matrices. As in the usual first-order transition matrix, the rows of the matrix refer to the antecedents and the columns refer to the consequents. However, in the second-order matrix the antecedents are now *pairs* of responses. In the first-order matrix that was generated for our example, A and B were possible antecedents responses. For the second-order matrix for this data, AA, AB, BA and BB are the antecedents—each of these pairs of responses being a possible two-response sequence preceding each of the possible consequents (A or B). For a third-order matrix, the antecedents become triplets of A and B responses—AAA, AAB, ABA, ABB, BAA, BAB, BBA, BBB. Table 12-1 presents the first-, second-, and third-order transitions for the two-category response sequence given earlier.

The procedure for testing the order of dependency (influence) among responses is essentially to test a series of models of dependency in which the number of antecedent responses on which the responses in the sequence are considered dependent is increased by one response in each subsequent test. That is, a first-order dependency model is compared to a random (zero-order) model with respect to its "goodness of fit" to the contingency data; a second-order model is compared with the first-order model; a third-order model is compared with the second-order model, and so on. For purposes of these tests, the contingency tables (see Table 12-1) serve as the data base for analysis. There are two methods generally used to estimate the goodness of fit of the interaction data to the various possible models (orders) of dependency: the chi square approach and the log-linear maximum likelihood approach.

TABLE 12-1

FIRST-, SECOND-, AND THIRD-ORDER CONTINGENCY TABLES
FOR THE TWO-CATEGORY SEQUENCE

First-order
contingencies

		t A	t B
t-1	A	7 (.44)[a]	9 (.56)
	B	8 (.62)	5 (.38)

Second-order
contingencies

		t-1	t A — A	t A — B	t B — A	t B — B
t-2	A		3	4	4	5
	B		4	4	4	0

Third-order
contingencies

t-3	t-2	t-1	t A — A	t A — B	t B — A	t B — B
	A	A	0	2	3	2
A		B	2	4	2	0
	B	A	3	0	2	3
B		B	2	0	2	0

[a]Values in parentheses are the first-order transition probabilities.

The first approach is based on a comparison of the observed and expected frequencies of each possible transition for each consecutive increase in the order of dependency. The difference between these values is then subjected to a chi square goodness of fit test for determining which model best describes the contingency relationships among the data. The most parsimonious model having a non-significant chi square value is generally considered to be the best-fitting model, and the order of dependency (number of antecedent responses) of that model may be said to describe the pattern of influence of that interaction sequence (Chatfield, 1973).

The log-linear maximum likelihood approach is similar to the chi square approach, but it uses the log-linear ratio statistic (G^2) rather than the chi square statistic. Generally speaking, the maximum likelihood approach is considered the better of these two alternatives (Bishop, Fienberg & Holland, 1975), but both are susceptible to difficulties associated with the chi square when they are applied to complex data models. In particular, as the order of dependency to be tested increases in number, the number of possible combinations of antecedent responses on which the various consequents can be contingent increases in a multiplicative fashion. Unless the number of actual events in the interaction sequence is quite large, this results in an increase in the number of empty cells in the contingency tables, thus weakening the power of the statistical tests (Chatfield & Lemon, 1973).

Lag Sequential Analysis

An alternative to the Markov model approach is the lag sequential analysis method (Sackett, 1979). As presented by Sackett, the particular advantage of this technique is that it allows for obtaining measures of contingency among events that are far apart in an interaction sequence without the concern for low-frequency cells. In this method of analysis, the concept of "lag" is essentially analogous to that of the "order of dependency" in the Markov models. It differs from this view, however, in that rather than considering the order of influence in terms of the number of antecedent responses preceding the consequent response, the order of influence is defined in terms of the number of lags (steps) *after* the occurrence of a response (antecedent) that the influence "takes effect." For example, the effect of a counselor's interpretive remark on a client may not be immediate but instead may reveal itself later on in the interaction of an interview or perhaps even in a later interview.

The basic procedure for lag analysis is as follows: Each response code in the counseling interaction serves as a "criterion" or starting point for determining the possible influence of the various responses on each other. For each specified criterion response code, the conditional probability of occurrence of each of the other response codes (including itself) is calculated as a function of the successive lags (steps) of each code from the criterion.

The response code sequence that we used as an example in the previous Markov model section can be used as an example here. To start, response code A is initially selected as the criterion. The next step in the procedure is to determine the number of times that each response code (including A) follows the criterion as the next response in the sequence (lag 1), as the second response following the criterion (lag 2), as the third response following the criterion (lag 3) and so on up to the largest sequential step (lag) of interest. Table 12-2 gives both the frequencies and the probabilities of occurrence of each response following each of the two possible criteria (A and B) up through lag 5.

TABLE 12-2

LAG MATCHING FREQUENCIES AND PROBABILITIES FOR THE
TWO-CATEGORY SEQUENCE

Lag	Number of Matched Occurrences			Probability	
	A	B	Total	A	B
Overall(unconditional)	16	14	30	.53	.47
A as criterion					
1	7	9	16	.44	.56
2	7	8	15	.47	.53
3	8	7	15	.53	.47
4	5	9	14	.36	.64
5	8	5	13	.62	.38
B as criterion					
1	8	5	13	.62	.38
2	7	5	12	.58	.42
3	6	6	12	.50	.50
4	8	4	12	.67	.33
5	5	7	12	.42	.58

Having determined these conditional lag probabilities, they can be tested for statistical significance against the null hypothesis of equivalence to the unconditional probabilities of the responses. Sackett (1979) proposes the binomial test as the appropriate method of testing for a statistically reliable difference between these probabilities. In this case the difference between the observed (conditional) lag probability of a response and the expected (unconditional) probability, when divided by the standard deviation of the expected probability, yields a standardized difference (Z) between these two probabilities.

The lack of a statistically reliable difference between the two probabilities suggests independence of those responses at that lag. If the standardized difference (Z) between the unconditional and the lag/conditional probability of a response at a given lag equals or exceeds an absolute value of 1.96, then the difference may be considered statistically reliable (p < .05). When the difference is positive, it suggests that the criterion response has an "excitatory effect" on the occurrence of the consequent response at that lag. When the difference is negative, the criterion may be said to have an "inhibitory effect" on the occurrence of the consequent response at that lag.

Lag analysis is particularly well suited for examining social interaction sequences for the remote or indirect influence of various response occurrences on the likelihood of occurrence of more distant responses (including its own recurrence). The approach also may be used to identify response patterns that may be generated by the constraint inherent in the interaction process. The process for identifying such patterns is referred to by Gottman (1979) as the "lag - one connection rule." Starting with some preselected response code as the criterion (typically the response code with the highest unconditional probability of occurrence), the investigator selects for the possible next response in the pattern the response code with the highest lag - 1 conditional probability from the criterion. Next, the investigator selects that response code with the highest lag - 2 probability from the criterion, the highest lag-3 probability, and so on. Using the lag data summarized in Table 12-2, the generated probable pattern of influence (up through lag - 5) would be A-B-B-A-B-A.

It is important to note that this pattern of responses is a likely pattern only if the lag - 1 probability from response 2 to response 3 is the highest conditional probability for that two-response sequence (with the second response now serving as the criterion). This process of verification of the various lag - 1 connections continues along the entire sequence, successively checking to be certain that each response is the most probable next response to its criterion.

The last step in identifying a response pattern is to assure that each conditional lag probability differs significantly from the simple unconditional likelihood of its occurrence. Even if a response is the most likely response at some lag from the criterion, if it is not more probable than its unconditional probability then it should be dropped from the pattern.

Information Theory

Information theory (Shannon & Weaver, 1949) offers yet another approach to the study of influence within social interaction processes. Social interaction may be characterized by some degree of redundancy between 0 and 100 percent. Redundancy in this sense is essentially synonymous with the notion of constraint or contingency among responses in the interaction sequence. In a larger sense it refers to the patterning among responses that emerges within the interaction as a consequence of that constraint. At the zero-order redundancy extreme, all responses in the interaction have an equal likelihood of occurrence — the history of the interaction prior to any given response has no effect on the predictability of the response. That is to say, there is complete uncertainty with respect to the patterning or occurrence of the various responses; or even more specifically, there is no patterning at all of the interaction responses. At the other extreme — that of 100 percent redundancy — the interaction sequence is completely predictable and a person can predict with certainty what each subsequent response will be.

The application of information theory to the study of interpersonal influence and the interaction patterning it creates consists of calculating the average conditional uncertainty for the counselor-client interaction for differing lengths of antecedent response sequences. The decrease in the uncertainty (an increase in redundancy) as the number of antecedent events increases may then be used to assess the extent of the dependency among the responses in the interaction sequence. A sequence evidences redundancy whenever some of the possible patterns of successive responses are more probable than others. The order of redundancy and the order of dependency are similar but not synonymous. Specifically, the order of redundancy is always one greater than the order of redundancy. The reason for this difference is as follows: Whereas the Markov model and lag-sequential analysis approaches are based on the difference between the conditional and unconditional probabilities of occurrence of responses in the sequence, information theory recognizes that a degree of "patterning" among responses will occur simply because of differences in the unconditional probabilities of the responses. For example, based simply on the unconditional probabilities of occurrence of A and B in our interaction sequence example, we are able to predict a "pattern" of more A's than B's occurring within the sequence (first-order redundancy) irrespective of knowledge of the preceding responses. Recall that only when all the responses have an equal likelihood of occurrence is there no redundancy. To the extent that the unconditional probabilities of occurrence of the various responses are not equal, a person may assume some degree of redundancy/patterning among those responses. Additionally, to the extent that some degree of influence (dependency) exists among responses in the social interaction, the likelihood of occurrence of the responses will change depending on which response(s) precede(s) them. Accompanying that change will be a change in the patterning of responses (and order of redundancy) that describes the response sequence. Identifying the nature of the influence within the social interaction consists of finding the degree of redundancy that best describes that interaction.

To calculate the degree of redundancy of patterning in a social interaction sequence, a decision must first be made concerning how high an order of redundancy one wishes to take into account. In a process similar to that in the analysis of Markov models, determination of the order of redundancy involves calculating the average conditional uncertainty for successive orders of redundancy and subtracting the average uncertainty of the previous order (Attneave, 1959). The difference between successive values of conditional uncertainty provides a measure of how much information is gained (i.e. how much uncertainty is reduced) by basing predictions for given responses on the previous n responses, rather than the previous $n - 1$ responses. The statistical significance of the successive changes in one's ability to predict responses can be tested by using a chi square approximation approach (Chatfield, 1973).

Table 12-3 presents the conditional uncertainty for the sample interaction sequence for patterns of one through four responses. The value H is the information theory measure of average uncertainty (Losey, 1978). The maximum value of H (when the responses are all equally likely—i.e. when redundancy is zero) is equal to the $\log_2$ of the number of response categories. In this instance the number of response categories is 2; therefore, $H = \log_2 2 = 1.0$. In the actual response sequence, however, the two responses are not equally likely to occur $[p(A) = .53$

and $p(B) = .47$] — although they are nearly equal. Because of the unequal distribution of A's and B's in the sequence, H does not achieve its maximum. The average uncertainty for A and B taken singularly (i.e. without considering prior response occurrences) is $H_1 = .991$. In a similar manner, the average (conditional) uncertainty may be computed across each of the possible two-response (digram), three-response (trigram), four-response (tetragram) and n-response (n-gram) patterns of responses which could occur within the interaction sequence. The amount of information (reduction in uncertainty) achieved by considering successively longer patterns of prior responses is determined by subtracting H_1 from H_2, H_2 from H_3, and so on.

TABLE 12-3

CONDITIONAL UNCERTAINTY FOR THE TWO-CATEGORY
SEQUENCE FOR SUCCESSIVE LEVELS OF DEPENDENCY

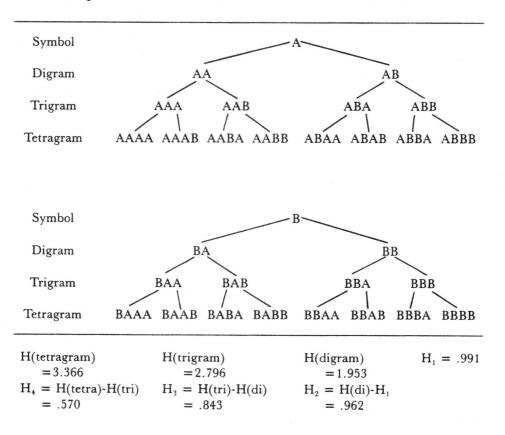

H(tetragram)	H(trigram)	H(digram)	$H_1 = .991$
$= 3.366$	$= 2.796$	$= 1.953$	
$H_4 = $ H(tetra)-H(tri)	$H_3 = $ H(tri)-H(di)	$H_2 = $ H(di)-H_1	
$= .570$	$= .843$	$= .962$	

Conclusion

The issue of influence within counseling, at least from a "process" perspective (Olson & Cromwell, 1975), is premised on the assumption of response interdependency between the counselor and the client. Counselors influence the responses of their clients to the extent that the counselors' responses either increase or decrease the occurrence of clients' responses over and above their simple unconditional probability of occurrence. And similarly, clients influence the responses of their counselors to the extent that the clients' responses result in an increase or decrease in the counselors' responses over and above their unconditional likelihood of occurrence.

This chapter has been an overview of three different methodological approaches to the investigation of social influence patterns within counseling interaction. While the actual use of these approaches in counseling process research is just beginning, we believe that these methods hold considerable promise for investigating the *process* of social influence and its relationship to counseling outcome.

CHAPTER 13

SOME REFLECTIONS ON THE INTERPERSONAL INFLUENCE PROCESS IN COUNSELING

P. Paul Heppner, Monica M. Menne,
and Joan I. Rosenberg

HELPING CLIENTS cope with and solve their personal problems is central to counseling and psychotherapy (Fretz, 1982; Krumboltz, 1965). There are many questions, however, regarding the avenues therapists may take to most effectively assist clients in coping with their problems. One central question pertains to how a counselor can facilitate change in clients. More specifically, what variables and processes are involved when a counselor affects a client to favorably alter specific opinions, attitudes, and behaviors? Strong (1968) initially conceptualized counseling as an interpersonal influence process by integrating research findings in social and counseling psychology. Since that time considerable attention within the counseling literature has been given to the interpersonal influence process (see Corrigan et al., 1980; Heppner & Dixon, 1981). In short, the "pace of the work has continued unabated" (Borgen, 1984).

In a previous paper (Heppner, Menne, & Rosenberg, 1985), we reviewed the interpersonal influence literature within counseling since the last reviews on this topic (Corrigan et al., 1980; Heppner & Dixon, 1981). The recent research has (a) increased our understanding of the type of events that effect clients' perceptions of counselor expertness, attractiveness, and trustworthiness, and (b) provided new information about the role of client characteristics in the influence process. The majority of the research, however, consists of data collected in situations of

137

questionable generalizability, with 44 percent (17 of 39) of the studies based on only 10.5 minutes of stimulus material.

The main purpose of this chapter is to reflect on the interpersonal influence literature and discuss some of our most salient concerns regarding the research and theory on the social influence literature within counseling. It is our belief that it may be useful to consider limits in our present knowledge of the social influence process in counseling and to subsequently identify possible directions for future research. Perhaps in this way, variables other than those previously examined may be investigated under the umbrella of the influence process in counseling, and, as a consequence, other models of influence may be developed. Our discussion of possible future research directions will center on four general themes: client-counselor characteristics, client information-processing, the complex *process* of counseling, and type of therapeutic interventions.

First, a substantial portion of the research has attended to establishing a greater understanding of the first stage of Strong's (1968) two-stage model of counseling (i.e. how counselors might enhance their perceived expertness, attractiveness, and trustworthiness). The influence process beyond the initial impressions of the counselor is relatively unknown; therefore, more investigations into the second stage, or how counselors use their influence to precipitate change, is needed. Subsequently, it is necessary to examine real-life counseling situations that involve: (a) actual counselors, (b) clients who have distressing problems they are motivated to examine, and (c) multiple sessions which extend over time.

With regard to psychometric issues, the Counselor Rating Form (CRF) (Barak & LaCrosse, 1975) is the most widely used assessment instrument within the social influence literature. There have been some questions raised about the statistical independence of the three factors: expertness, attractiveness, and trustworthiness (see Ponterotto & Furlong, 1985). Additional research is needed to examine the independence or interdependence of these constructs in the perceptual processes of clients. With intercorrelations typically ranging between .7 and .8 among the three factors, perhaps half the variance accounts for a perception of a general halo effect of the counselor. But beyond that it may be useful to partial out distinct variance attributable to expertness, attractiveness, or trustworthiness.

With regard to counselor characteristics, it is unknown which counselor behaviors or cues account for the most variance on perceived expertness, attractiveness, and trustworthiness either in the first session or throughout multiple sessions. Does the effect of objective evidence of training (e.g. diplomas) or counselor physical attractiveness persist over time? Existing evidence suggests that certain nonverbal and verbal behaviors may be weighted more strongly than other cues in the initial stages of counseling (e.g. Barak, Patkin, & Dell, 1982). Anecdotal evidence reported at the end of counseling indicates that clients base their perceptions of the counselor on specific counselor behaviors or identifiable therapeutic changes within the client (e.g. Heppner & Heesacker, 1982).

To what extent initial perceptions of a counselor are based on legitimate power, versus expert or referent power (see French & Raven, 1959), is unknown. There is considerable evidence that a wide variety of counselors are typically rated as quite expert, attractive, and trustworthy based on a minimal amount of stimulus material (analogue studies) or after one counseling session (e.g. Atkinson, Brady, & Casas, 1981; Heppner & Heesacker, 1982; McKitrick, 1981; Zamostny, Corrigan, & Eggert, 1981), which seems to support legitimate power sources. If initial impressions of counselors are strongly related to legitimate power, perhaps a counselor is assumed expert and trustworthy until proven otherwise. But how long does legitimate power exist? What does it take for a counselor's legitimate power base to be diminished? What constitutes a significant reduction? What are the consequences of a major decrease in this source of power?

Likewise, it is unknown to what extent *actual* expert or skillful counselor performance affects the influence process. Strong (1968) initially focused on perceived counselor resources (e. g. expertness), and later investigations have examined specific aspects of the counselor (e.g. attire, diplomas) and the counselor role (e.g. reputation). Thus, researchers have often attended to how the counselor "appears to be" to the client, rather than focusing on whether the counselor is or is not exhibiting real expertise (see Harmon, 1984). Thus, it may be worthwhile to examine the effect of real rather than perceived expertness. Perhaps, one methodological strategy would be to examine differences in the influence process between a very skillful as opposed to a novice counselor throughout the course of counseling, examining differences in conceptualization, diagnoses, communication and intervention skills.

Also, it is unknown if the influence process differs for clients with very different presenting problems, personality patterns, or clinical diagnoses. The uniformity myth has not been questioned within the interpersonal influence literature. Is the influence process different for a person with a long-standing personality disorder as opposed to a person with a more developmental skill deficit?

Similarly, it is unknown if client characteristics, such as perceived need to change, involvement, opposition, or resistance, affect how clients process information within counseling. There is some suggestive evidence that opposition and resistance do differentially affect the influence process (e.g. Kerr et al., 1983). What counseling activities and strategies, therefore, would be most useful for clients who have varying levels of resistance and opposition, especially as counseling progresses?

It is possible that a client's experience level in counseling may also affect the social influence process. What counselor characteristic or message variables might account for more variance in influence attempts for novice as opposed to experienced clients?

It is also likely that some clients may be influenced in the counseling process without correctly attributing causality to the counselor. Nisbett and Wilson (1977) provide evidence that people have difficulty accurately reporting their internal cognitive/sensory/perceptual processes in ambiguous situations; for many clients, counseling and the change process may be quite ambiguous. Therefore, due to the difficulty in discriminating and reporting changes in one's process, ratings other than just those by clients may be needed to investigate the influence process. In short, it must be questioned whether clients are able to accurately report significant perceptual/cognitive changes they have made through contact with the counselor. In addition, relying solely on client reports provides a very narrow view of client "change" (see Highlen & Hill, 1984). Client change is a multi-faceted, complex process that may best be examined through a wide variety of modalities.

Research on the influence process in counseling should be integrated with findings from counseling-outcome research. Orlinsky and Howard (1978) concluded that the positive quality of the "relationship bond" between counselor and client was related to client improvement more so than any treatment techniques used by counselors. A number of practitioners and theoreticians also have pointed to the "therapeutic relationship" as a key ingredient in the counseling process (Gelso & Carter, 1985; Goldfried, 1980; Highlen & Hill, 1984). Gelso and Carter (1985) have proposed three components of the therapeutic relationship: the working alliance, transference, and the real relationship. It is clear that various components of the therapeutic relationship are related to counseling outcomes. Therefore, it may be quite fruitful to integrate findings regarding components of the therapeutic relationship into the research on perceived expertness, attractiveness, and trustworthiness. In particular, it may be useful to examine the function of the three components identified by Gelso and Carter (1985) (across theoretical systems and clients) in relationship to the influence process.

It is unknown how clients process information within the counseling process which may either enhance or decrease the probability of bringing about therapeutic changes. Do influence attempts need to be made repeatedly? And over time? And at particular times? What variables (counselor perceptions vs. message characteristics) have more impact on how clients process information within and between counseling sessions? Whereas various persuasion models have been developed in social psychology (e.g. the Elaboration-Likelihood Model) (Petty & Cacioppo, 1981), there has been little testing of the generalizability of these models within real-life counseling. Likewise, much more could be done in applying information-processing models (e.g. Anderson, 1983) to understanding how clients process the counseling experience. For example, Dixon (1986) has creatively applied Janis and Mann's (1977) decision-making model to understanding the client processing of information related to resistance and change. In short, more attention is needed to understand how clients process the counseling experience, particularly as counseling relates to client change.

It may also be useful to integrate process-oriented research techniques to measure aspects of the change process. At present, the process research in counseling is moving away from isolating specific static events and toward the examination of a broad range of counselor activities as they interact with client characteristics (Highlen & Hill, 1984; Hill, 1982). The identification of factors that affect client change are increasing, and the models of the counseling process are acknowledging the highly interactive, reciprocal nature of counseling (Highlen & Hill, 1984). The influence literature could capitalize on the recent advances in process research by incorporating their theoretical models, methodological procedures, and instrumentation. For example, Elliott (1981) has maintained that clients weigh some counselor-client interactions more than others, and that it is useful to evaluate critical incidents or major turning points within counseling. It may be particularly interesting to note how such critical incidents might relate to the influence process.

Additionally, within the social influence paradigm, it is unknown which counselor interventions may be most influential with clients, initially as well as throughout the counseling process. Investigators are beginning to examine some interventions, such as interpretations or paradoxical statements (e.g. Beck & Strong, 1982; Claiborn, 1982; Claiborn, Crawford, & Hackman, 1983; Claiborn, Ward & Strong,

1981; Feldman, Strong, & Danser, 1982; Kerr et al., 1983), but much more remains to be done. (This research is in contrast to the wealth of research on counseling interventions in general; the point here is that research on counseling interventions has not been examined as extensively within the social influence literature.) What interventions affect client change, apart from or in addition to affecting client perceptions of the counselor? A broad range of intervention strategies need to be examined with the social influence paradigm, particularly those that increase clients' feelings of self-worth, mastery of their environment, cognitive and experiential learning, self-awareness, and expectations of help (i.e. hope). It is essential that the short and long-term effects of different interventions are examined across different times in the counseling process. For example, a colleague noted that congruent interpretations seem to be more useful early in the relationship building phase of counseling, whereas incongruent or challenging interpretations are more functional later in counseling.*

Finally, the steps a client experiences during various therapeutic changes, and how relatively simple versus complex client goals affect the influence process, is unknown. For example, how do clients decide if they are progressing or satisfied with counseling, and how does this then affect the influence process later in counseling? It may be useful to examine sub-goals within the counseling process (e.g. establishing a relationship, awareness and knowledge of self, perceived goals in counseling, symptom reduction, skill acquisition) as important steps in the influence process.

Conclusions

How different clients change through counseling is not a simple, unitary, uniform process. The variables and processes involved when a counselor favorably affects a client to alter specific opinions, attitudes, and behaviors is not totally clear at this time. A considerable amount of research has examined this question from an interpersonal influence perspective since Strong (1968) initially conceptualized counseling as an influence process. Our knowledge base of the influence process in counseling has certainly been increased since 1968. In addition, more complex theoretical issues have been advanced (e.g. Claiborn, 1982; Strong & Claiborn, 1982). Likewise, the research has increased in complexity

---

*N. Downing 1984: personal communication.

and sophistication. However, we have only scratched the surface. The vast majority of studies have examined only the initial phase of counseling and is based primarily on analogue research. Therefore, the generalizability to extended contact in real-life counseling is questionable.

Important advances in the understanding of the interpersonal influence process at this time can be made if two critical issues are taken into consideration. First, research in this area *must move away from the overutilization of analogue methodologies* and, instead, experimental field designs must be incorporated. It is necessary that the interpersonal influence process be examined in actual counseling situations over time. Variations in design strategies are also encouraged (e.g. single subject). If analogue methodologies are used, it is imperative that, at the very least, three of Strong's (1971) boundary conditions be incorporated into the study (conversation between two people with a status differential over time).

Secondly, we have suggested a number of research directions and we propose that *a wider range of variables be examined in the influence process.* This includes variables involving actual counselor expertise, the cognitive processes of clients, the relationship bond, client characteristics including diagnoses, and a number of counseling outcomes (e.g. awareness of self). Furthermore, the interpersonal influence research could benefit by integrating findings from counseling process and outcome research. Likewise, it has been suggested that the influence process may differ across counselors and clients, and that an attribute-treatment-interaction approach (ATI, Fretz, 1981) be adopted.

Rather than just identifying components of perceived counselor expertness, attractiveness, and trustworthiness, the most critical next step is to examine the interactional aspects of change processes (Highlen & Hill, 1984; Strong & Claiborn, 1982). Creative approaches are needed to develop suitable assessment instruments, to tailor methodologies to our unique research problems, and to isolate critical variables through rigor while avoiding artificial abstractions. Five to ten years from now, we should be able to assess how much we have learned not only about the influence process but also hopefully about the process and outcome of counseling in general.

BIBLIOGRAPHY

Adler, A. (1956). *The Individual Psychology of Alfred Adler.* H. L. Ansbacher & R. R. Ansbacher (Eds.). New York: Basic Books.

Anchin, J. (1982). Sequence, pattern and style: Integration and treatment implications of some interpersonal concepts. In J. Anchin & D. Kiesler (Eds.), *Handbook of interpersonal psychotherapy.* New York: Pergamon.

Anderson, J. R. (1983). *The architecture of cognition.* Cambridge: Harvard University Press.

Anderson, C. M., & Stewart, S. (1983). *Mastering resistance: A practical guide to family therapy.* New York: Guilford.

Atkinson, D. R., Brady, S., & Casas, J. M. (1981). Sexual preference similarity, attitude similarity, and perceived counselor credibility and attractiveness. *Journal of Counseling Psychology, 28,* 504-509.

Atkinson, D., & Wampold, B. (1982). A comparison of the counselor rating form and the counselor effectiveness scale. *Counselor Education and Supervision, 22,* 25-36.

Atkinson, D., & Carskadden, G. (1975). A prestigious introduction, psychological jargon, and perceived counselor credibility. *Journal of Counseling Psychology, 22,* 180-186.

Attneave, F. (1959). *Applications of information theory to psychology.* New York: Holt.

Baekland, F., & Lundwall, L. (1975). Dropping out of treatment: A critical review. *Psychological Bulletin, 82,* 738-783.

Bandura, A. (1977). Self-efficacy: Toward a unifying theory of behavioral change. *Psychological Review, 84,* 191-215.

Bandura, A. (1982). Self efficacy mechanism in human agency. *American Psychologist, 37,* 122-147.

Barak, A., & Dell, D. (1977). Differential perceptions of counselor behavior. *Journal of Counseling Psychology, 24,* 288-292.

Barak, A., & Lacrosse, M. B. (1975). Multidimensional perception of counselor behavior. *Journal of Counseling Psychology, 22,* 471-476.

Barak, A., Patkin, J., & Dell, D. (1982). Effects of certain counselor behaviors on perceived expertness and attractiveness. *Journal of Counseling Psychology, 29,* 261-267.

Beck, J. T., & Strong, S. R. (1982). Stimulating therapeutic change with interpretations: A comparison of positive and negative connotation. *Journal of Counseling Psychology, 29,* 551-559.

Beier, E. G. (1966). *The silent language of psychotherapy.* Chicago: Aldine.

Bem, D. J. (1968). Dissonance reduction in the behaviorist. In R. Abelson, E. Aronson, W. McGuire, T. Newcomb, M. Rosenberg, & P. Tannenbaum (Eds.), *Theories of cognitive consistency: A sourcebook* (pp. 246-256). Chicago: Rand McNally.

Bergin, A. (1971). The evaluation of therapeutic outcomes. In Bergin, A. and Garfield, S. (Eds.), *Handbook of Psychotherapy and Behavior Change.* New York: Wiley.

Betz, N. E., & Shullman, S. L. (1979). Factors related to client return rate following intake. *Journal of Counseling Psychology, 26,* 542-545.

Bieber, M. R. (1978). *A language analysis of three counseling series.* Unpublished doctoral dissertation, University of Utah, Salt Lake City.

Bieber, M. R., Patton, M. J., & Fuhriman, A. J. (1977). A metalanguage analysis of counselor and client verb usage in counseling. *Journal of Counseling Psychology, 24,* 264-271.

Billings, M., & Dixon, D. N. (1984, August). *Prediction of parent training outcomes from pre-commitment variables.* Paper presented at meeting of the American Psychological Association, Toronto.

Bishop, Y., Fienberg, S., & Holland, P. (1975). *Discrete multivariate analysis.* Cambridge, MA: MIT Press.

Borgen, F. H. (1984). Counseling psychology. In M. R. Rosenzweig & L. W. Porter (Eds.), *Annual review of psychology*: Vol. 35 (pp. 579-604). California: Annual Reviews Inc.

Brehm, S. (1976). *The application of social psychology to clinical practice.* New York: Wiley.

Cacioppo, J. T., & Petty, R. E. (1984). The need for cognition: Relationship to attitudinal processes. In R. P. McGlynn, J. E. Maddux, C. D. Stoltenberg, & J. H. Harvey (Eds.), *Social perception in clinical and counseling psychology* (pp. 113-139). Lubbock, TX: Texas Tech Press.

Cacioppo, J. T., & Petty, R. E. (1982). The need for cognition. *Journal of Personality and Social Psychology, 42,* 116-131.

Cacioppo, J. T., & Petty, R. E. (1981). Social psychological procedures for cognitive response assessment. In T. Merluzzi, C. Glass, & M. Genest (Eds.), *Cognitive assessment* (pp. 309-342). New York: Guilford.

Cacioppo, J. T., & Petty, R. E. (1979). Effects of message repetition and position on cognitive responses, recall, and persuasion. *Journal of Personality and Social Psychology, 37,* 97-109.

Cacioppo, J. T., Harkins, S. G., & Petty, R. E. (1981). The nature of attitudes and cognitive responses and their relationships to behavior. In R. R. Petty, T. M. Ostrum, & T. C. Brock (Eds.), *Cognitive responses in persuasion* (pp. 31-54). Hillsdale, NJ: Erlbaum.

Cacioppo, J. T., & Petty, R. E., & Morris, K. J. (1983). Effects of need for cognition of message evaluation, recall, and persuasion. *Journal of Personality and Social Psychology, 45,* 805-818.

Cacioppo, J. T., Petty, R. E., & Stoltenberg, C. D. (1984). Processes of social influence: The elaboration likelihood model of persuasion. In P. Kendall (Eds.), *Advances in cognitive-behavioral research and practice.* New York: Academic Press.

Carson, R. (1969). *Interaction concepts of personality.* Chicago: Aldine.

Carter, J. A. (1978). Impressions of counselors as a function of counselor physical attractiveness. *Journal of Counseling Psychology, 25,* 28-34.

Cash, T. F., Begley, P. J., McCown, D. A., & Wise, B. C. (1975). When counselors are heard but not seen: Initial impact of physical attractiveness. *Journal of Counseling Psychology, 22,* 273-279.

Cash, T. F., & Derleg, V. J. (1978). The matching hypothesis; Physical attractiveness among same-sexed friends. *Personality and Social Psychology Bulletin, 4,* 24-243.

Cash, T. F., Gillen, B., & Burns, D. S. (1977). Sexism and "beautism" in personnel consultant decision making. *Journal of Applied Psychology, 62,* 301-310.

Cash, T. F., & Kehr, J. (1978). Influence of nonprofessional counselors' physical attractiveness and sex on perceptions of counselor behavior. *Journal of Counseling Psychology, 25,* 336-342.

Chaiken, S. (1980). Heuristic versus systematic information processing and the use of source versus message cues in persuasion. *Journal of Personality and Social Psychology, 39,* 752-766.

Chatfield, C. (1973). Statistical inference regarding Markov chain models. *Applied Statistics, 22,* 7-20.

Chatfield, C., & Lemon, R. (1970). Analyzing sequences of behavioral events. *Journal of Theoretical Biology, 29,* 427-445.

Cialdini, R. B., Petty, R. E., & Cacioppo, J. T. (1981). Attitudes and attitude change. *Annual Review of Psychology, 32,* 357-404.

Claiborn, C. D. (1982). Interpretation and change in counseling. *Journal of Counseling Psychology, 29,* 439-453.

Claiborn, C. D. (1979). Counselor verbal intervention, nonverbal behavior, and social power. *Journal of Counseling Psychology, 26,* 378-383.

Claiborn, C. D., Crawford, J. B., & Hackman, H. W. (1983). Effects of intervention discrepancy in counseling for negative emotions. *Journal of Counseling Psychology, 30,* 164-171.

Claiborn, C. D., Ward, S. R., & Strong, S. R. (1981). Effects of congruence between counselor interpretations and client beliefs. *Journal of Counseling Psychology, 28,* 101-109.

Claiborn, C. D., & Schmidt, L. (1977). Effects of presession information on the perception of the counselor in an interview. *Journal of Counseling Psychology, 24,* 259-263.

Cohen, A. R., & Latane, B. (1962). An experiment on choice in commitment to counterattitudinal behavior. In J. W. Brehm & A. R. Cohen, *Explorations in cognitive dissonance.* New York: Wiley, 88-91.

Cook, W. A. (1979). *Case grammar: Development of the matrix model (1970-1978).* Washington, D. C.: Georgetown University Press.

Corrigan, J. D., Dell, D. M., Lewis, K. N., & Schmidt, L. D. (1980). Counseling as a social influence process: A review. *Journal of Counseling Psychology, 27,* 395-441.

Corrigan, J., & Schmidt, L. (1983). Development and validation of revisions in the counselor rating form. *Journal of Counseling Psychology, 30,* 64-75.

Crowder, J. E. (1972). Relationship between therapist and client interpersonal behaviors and psychotherapy outcome. *Journal of Counseling Psychology, 19,* 68-75.

Croyle, R., & Cooper, J. (1983). Dissonance arousal: Physiological evidence. *Journal of Personality and Social Psychology, 45,* 782-791.

Cutler, R. L. (1958). Countertransference effects in psychotherapy. *Journal of Consulting Psychology, 22,* 349-356.

Davis, D., Cook, D., Jennings, R., & Heck, E. (1977). Differential client attractiveness in a counseling analogue. *Journal of Counseling Psychology, 24,* 472-476.

Dell, D., & Schmidt, L. (1976). Expert and inexpert counselors. *Journal of Counseling Psychology, 23,* 197-201.

Dell, D. (1973). Counselor power base, influence attempt, and behavior change in counseling. *Journal of Counseling Psychology, 20,* 399-405.

Dietzel, C. S., & Abeles, N. (1975). Client-therapist complementarity and therapeutic outcome. *Journal of Counseling Psychology, 22,* 264-272.

Dinkmeyer, D., Pew, W. L., & Dinkmeyer, D., Jr. (1979). *Adlerian counseling and psychotherapy.* Monterey, CA: Brooks/Cole.

Dion, K. K., Berscheid, E., & Walster, E. (1972). What is beautiful is good. *Journal of Personality and Social Psychology, 24,* 285-290.

Dipboye, R. L., Fromkin, H. L., & Wiback, K. (1975). Relative importance of applicant sex, attractiveness, and scholastic standing in evaluation of job applicant resumes. *Journal of Applied Psychology, 60,* 39-43.

Dixon, D. N., Bukacek, S. E., Govaerts, K. A., Kerr, B. A., Lambert, D. J., Olson, D. H., & Sutton, C. S. (1983, August). *Resistance and treatment compliance: A social psychological analysis.* Symposium conducted at meeting of the American Psychological Association, Anaheim, CA.

Dixon, D. (1986). Client resistance and social influence. In F. J. Dorn (Ed.), *The social influence process in counseling and psychotherapy.* Springfield: Illinois: Charles C Thomas.

Dixon, D. N., & Claiborn, C. D. (1981). Effects of need and commitment on career exploration behaviors. *Journal of Counseling Psychology, 28,* 411-415.

Dorn, F. (1984a). The social influence model: A social-psychological approach to counseling. *Personnel and Guidance Journal, 62,* 342-345.

Dorn, F. (1984b). *Counseling as applied social psychology: An introduction to the social influence model.* Springfield, Illinois: Charles C Thomas.

Dorn, F. J. (1984). The social influence model: A cautionary note on counseling psychology's warm embrace. *Journal of Counseling Psychology, 31,* 111-115.

Dorn, F., & Jereb. R. (1985). Enhancing the useability of the counselor rating form for practitioners and researchers. *Measurement and Evaluation in Counseling and Development, 18,* 12-16.

Duckro, P., Beal, D., & George, C. (1979). Research on the effects of disconfirmed client role expectations in psychotherapy: A critical review. *Psychological Bulletin, 86,* 260-275.

Duehn, W. D., & Proctor, E. K. (1977). Initial clinical interaction and premature discontinuance in treatment. *American Journal of Orthopsychiatry, 47,* 284-290.

Eagly, A. H. (1967). Involvement as a determinant of response to favorable and unfavorable information. *Journal of Personality and Social Psychology, 7* (1-15, Whole No. 643).

Eagly, A. H. (1974). Comprehensibility of persuasive arguments as a determinant of opinion change. *Journal of Personality and Social Psychology, 29,* 758-773.

Eagly, A. H. (1981). Recipient characteristics as determinants of responses to persuasion. In R. E. Petty, T. M. Ostrom, & T. C. Brock (Eds.), *Cognitive responses in persuasion* (pp. 173-195). Hillsdale, NJ: Erlbaum.

Eagly, A. H. (1983). Gender and social influence: A social psychological analysis. *American Psychologist, 38,* 971-981.

Elliott, R. (1981). *Fitting process research to the working clinician.* EPIC/CAPS. Resources in Education.

Endler, N. S., & Magnusson, D. (1976). Personality and person by situation interactions. In N. S. Endler & D. Magnusson (Eds.), *Interactional psychology and personality* (pp. 1-25). Washington: Hemisphere.

Epperson, D. L., Bushway, D. J., & Warman, R. E. (1983). Client self-terminations after one counseling session: Effects of problem recognition, counselor gender, and counselor experience. *Journal of Counseling Psychology, 30,* 307-315.

Fazio, R. H., Zanna, M. P., Cooper, J. (1977). Dissonance and self-perception: An integrative view of each theory's proper domain of application. *Journal of Experimental Psychology, 15,* 464-479.

Feldman, D. A., Strong, S. R., & Danser, D. B. (1982). A comparison of paradoxical and nonparadoxical interpretations and directives. *Journal of Counseling Psychology, 29,* 572-579.

Fenichel, O. (1945). *The psychoanalytic theory of neurosis.* New York: W. W. Norton & Company, Inc.

Festinger, L. (1957). *A theory of cognitive dissonance.* Evanston, Ill: Row Peterson.

Forsyth, N., & Forsyth, D. (1982). Internality, controllability, and the effectiveness of attributional interpretations in counseling. *Journal of Counseling Psychology, 29,* 140-150.

Frank, J. D. (1973). *Persuasion and healing: A comparative study of psychotherapy* (2nd ed.). Baltimore, Md: Johns Hopkins University Press.

French, J., & Raven, B. (1959). The basis of social power. In D. Cartwright (Ed.), *Studies in social power.* Ann Arbor Institute of Social Research.

Fretz, B. R. (1981). Evaluating the effectiveness of career interventions. *Journal of Counseling Psychology, 28,* 77-90.

Fretz, B. R. (1982). Perspective and definitions. *The Counseling Psychologist, 10*(2), 15-20.

Freud, S. (1966). *Introductory lectures on psychoanalysis* (J. Strachey, Ed. and Trans.). New York: Norton. (Original work published, 1916-1917.)

Friedlander, M. L. (1984). Psychotherapy talk as social control. *Psychotherapy, 21,* 333-339.

Friedlander, M. L. & Phillips, S. D. (1984). A stochastic process analysis of interactive discourse in early counseling interviews. *Journal of Counseling Psychology, 31,* 139-148.

Friedman, H. J. (1963). Patient expectancy and symptom reduction. *Archives of General Psychiatry, 8,* 61-67.

Garfield, S. L. (1980). *Psychotherapy: An eclectic approach.* New York: Wiley.

Garfield, S. L. (1978). Research on client variables in psychotherapy. In S. L. Garfield & A. E. Bergin (Eds.), *Handbook of psychotherapy and behavior change: An empirical analysis* (2nd ed.). New York: Wiley.

Garfield, S. L., & Affleck, D. C. (1959). An appraisal of duration of stay in outpatient psychotherapy. *Journal of Nervous and Mental Disease, 129,* 492-498.

Geer, C. A., & Hurst, J. C. (1976). Counselor-subject sex variables in systematic desensitization. *Journal of Counseling Psychology, 23,* 296-301.

Gelso, C. (1979). Research in counseling: Methodological and professional issues. *The Counseling Psychologist, 8,* 7-36.

Gelso, C., & Carter, J. A. (1985). The relationship in counseling and psychotherapy: Components, consequences and theoretical antecedents. *The Counseling Psychologist, 13,* 155-243.

Goldfried, M. R. (1980). Some views on effective principles of psychotherapy. *Cognitive Therapy and Research, 4,* 269-306.

Goldman, L. (1978). Introduction and point of view. In L. Goldman (Ed.). *Research methods for counselors: Practical approaches in field settings* (pp. 3-26). New York: John Wiley and Sons.

Goldstein, A. (1966). Psychotherapy research by extrapolation from social psychology. *Journal of Counseling Psychology, 13,* 38-45.

Goldstein, A. P., Heller, K., & Sechrest, L. B. (1966), *Psychotherapy and the psychology of behavior change.* New York: Wiley.

Goodyear, R., Abadie, P., & Brunson, B. (1982). Counselor influence methods: Perceptions based on counselor and client ages. *AMHCA Journal, 4,* 78-88.

Goodyear, R., & Robyak, J. (1981). Counseling as an interpersonal influence process: A perspective for counseling practice. *Personnel and Guidance Journal, 60,* 654-657.

Gottman, J. (1979). *Marital interaction.* New York: Academic Press.

Guttman, M., & Haase, R. (1972). Effect of experimentally induced sets of high and low expertness during brief vocational counseling. *Counselor Education and Supervision, 11,* 171-178.

Hackman, H., & Claiborn C. (1982). An attributional approach to counselor attractiveness. *Journal of Counseling Psychology, 29,* 224-231.

Harmon, L. W. (1984). Thinking about the social influence model: A cautionary note in response to Dorn. *Journal of Counseling Psychology, 31,* 116-117.

Hector, M. A., Wyman, E. A., & Meara, N. M. (1984, April). The effects of semantic and stylistic variations in language on perception of social influence characteristics. In M. J. Patton (Chair), *Research on language analysis in counseling.* Session conducted at the annual meeting of the American Educational Research Association, New Orleans.

Heesacker, M., & Heppner, P. P. (1983). Using real client perceptions to examine psychometric properties of the counselor rating form. *Journal of Counseling Psychology, 30,* 180-187.

Heesacker, M., Heppner, P. P., & Rogers, M. (1982). Classics and emerging classics in counseling psychology. *Journal of Counseling Psychology, 29,* 400-405.

Heesacker, M., Petty, R. E., & Cacioppi, J. T. (1983). Source credibility can alter persuasion by affecting message-relevant thinking. *Journal of Personality, 51,* 653-666.

Heilbrun, A. B. (1982). Cognitive factors in early counseling termination: Social insight and level of defensiveness. *Journal of Counseling Psychology, 29*(1), 29-38.

Heppner, P. P., & Dixon, D. N. (1978). Effects of client perceived need and counselor role on clients' behavior. *Journal of Counseling Psychology, 25,* 514-519.

Heppner, P. P., & Dixon, D. (1981). A review of the interpersonal influence process in counseling. *Personnel and Guidance Journal, 59,* 542-550.

Heppner, P. P., & Heesacker, M. (1982). Interpersonal influence process in real-life counseling: Investigating client perceptions, counselor experience level, and counselor power over time. *Journal of Counseling Psychology, 29,* 215-223.

Heppner, P. P., Menne, M., & Rosenberg, J. (1985). *Evaluating the influence process in counseling: Data, thoughts, and questions.* Manuscript submitted for publication.

Heppner, P. P., & Pew, S. (1977). Effects of diplomas, awards, and counselor sex on perceived expertness. *Journal of Counseling Psychology, 24,* 147-149.

Highlen, P., & Hill, C. (1984). Factors affecting client change in individual counseling: Current status and theoretical speculation. In S. Brown & R. Lent (Eds.), *The handbook of counseling psychology.* New York: John Wiley.

Hill, C. E. (1983). An overview of the Hill counselor and client Verbal Response Modes Category Systems. In L. Greenberg & W. Piasof (Eds.), *Psychotherapeutic process: A research handbook.* New York: Guilford.

Hill, C. (1982). Counseling process research: Philosophical and methodological dilemmas. *The Counseling Psychologist, 10,* 7-19.

Hobbs, N. (1962). Sources of gain in psychotherapy. *American Psychologist, 17,* 741-747.

Hoffman-Graff, M. A. (1977). Interviewer use of positive and negative self-disclosure and interviewer-subject sex pairing. *Journal of Counseling Psychology, 24,* 184-190.

Hoffman, M., & Teglasi, H. (1982). The role of casual attributions in counseling shy subjects. *Journal of Counseling Psychology, 29,* 132-139.

Holland, J. L. (1973). *Making vocational choices: A theory of careers.* Englewood Cliffs, NJ: Prentice-Hall.

Holland, J. L. (1979). *Professional manual for the Self-Directed Search.* Palo Alto, CA: Counseling Psychologists Press.

Hovland, C. I., Janis, I. L., & Kelly, J. J. (1953). *Communication and persuasion: Psychological studies of opinion change.* New Haven, CT: Yale University Press.

Hundron, C., Pepinsky, H., & Meara, N. (1979). Conceptual level and structural complexity in language. *Journal of Counseling Psychology, 26,* 190-197.

Jaffe, J. (1964). Verbal behavior analysis in psychiatric interviews with the aid of digital computer. In D. M. K. Roch & E. A. Weinstein (Eds.), *Disorders of communication,* Vol. 42. Baltimore, MD: Williams & Wilkins.

Jahn, D., & Lichstein, K. (1980). The resistive client: A neglected phenomenon in behavior therapy. *Behavior Modification, 4,* 303-320.

Janis, I. L. & Mann, L. (1977). *Decision making: A psychological analysis of conflict, choice and commitment.* New York: Free Press.

Kaul, T. J., & Schmidt, L. D. (1971). Dimensions of interviewer trustworthiness. *Journal of Counseling Psychology, 18,* 542-548.

Kell, B. L., & Mueller, W. J. (1966). *Impact and change: A study of counseling relationships.* New York: Appleton-Century-Crofts.

Kerr, B. A., Claiborn, C. D., & Dixon, D. N. (1982). Training counselors in persuasion. *Counselor Education and Supervision, 22,* 138-148.

Kerr, B., & Dell, D. (1976). Perceived interviewer expertness and attractiveness: Effects of interviewer behavior and attire and interview setting. *Journal of Counseling Psychology, 23,* 553-556.

Kerr, B. A., Olson, D. H., Claiborn, C. D., Bauers-Gruenler, S. J., & Paolo, A. M. (1983). Overcoming opposition and resistance: Differential functions of expertness and attractiveness in career counseling. *Journal of Counseling Psychology, 30,* 323-331.

Kleinke, C. L., & Tully, T. B. (1979). Influence of talking level on perceptions of counselors. *Journal of Counseling Psychology, 26,* 23-29.

Krauskopf, C. J., Baumgarder, A., & Mandracehia, S. (1981). Return rate following intake revisited. *Journal of Counseling Psychology, 28,* 519-521.

Krumboltz, J. D. (1965). Behavioral counseling: Rationale and research. *Personnel and Guidance Journal, 44,* 383-387.

La Crosse, M. (1980). Perceived counselor influence and counseling outcomes: Validity of the counselor rating form. *Journal of Counseling Psychology, 27,* 320-327.

La Crosse, M. (1975). Nonverbal behavior and perceived counselor attractiveness and persuasiveness. *Journal of Counseling Psychology, 22,* 563-566.

La Crosse, M. & Barak, A. (1976). Differential perception of counselor behavior. *Journal of Counseling Psychology, 23,* 170-172.

Lambert, M., Stein, D., & DeJulio, S. (1978). Therapist interpersonal skills: Process, outcome, methodological considerations, and recommendation for future research. *Psychological Bulletin, 85,* 467-489.

Lambert, M. J., Christensen, E. R., & DeJulio, S. S. (1983). *The assessment of psychotherapy.* New York: Wiley.

Langs, R. (1980). *Resistance and interventions: The nature of therapeutic work.* New York: Aronson.

Leary, T. (1957). *Interpersonal diagnosis of personality.* New York: Ronald.

Lennard, H. L., & Bernstein, A. (1967). Role learning in psychotherapy. *Psychotherapy: Theory, Research, and Practice, 4,* 1-6.

Levy, L. H. (1963). *Psychological interpretation.* New York: Holt, Rinehart, & Winston, Inc.

Lewis, K., Davis, C., Walker, B., & Jennings, R. (1981). Attractive versus unattractive clients: Mediating influences on counselor's perceptions. *Journal of Counseling Psychology, 28,* 309-314.

Lewis, K. N., & Walsh, W. B. (1978). Physical attractiveness: Its impact on the perception of a female counselor. *Journal of Counseling Psychology, 25,* 210-216.

Lewis, K., & Walsh, B. (1980). Effects of value-communication style and similarity of values on counselor evaluation. *Journal of Counseling Psychology, 27,* 305-314.

Lichtenberg, J. W., & Hummel, T. J. (1976). Counseling as a stochastic process: Fitting a Markov chain model to initial counseling interviews. *Journal of Counseling Psychology, 23,* 310-315.

Lochman, J. E., & Brown, M. V. (1980). Evaluation of dropout clients and of perceived usefulness of a parent education program. *Journal of Community Psychology, 8,* 132-139.

Losey, G. (1978). Information theory and communication. In P. Colgan (Ed.), *Quantitative ethology.* New York: Wiley.

Luborsky, L., Chandler, M., Auerbach, A. H., Cohen, J., & Bachrach, H. M. (1971). Factors influencing the outcome of psychotherapy: A review of quantitative research. *Psychological Bulletin, 75,* 145-185.

McGinley, P. (1954). *Love letters.* NY: Viking Press.

McGuire, W. J. (1969). The nature of attitudes and attitude change. In G. Lindzey & Aronson (Eds.), *The handbook of social psychology.* Vol. 3, 2nd ed. Reading, MA: Addison-Wesley.

McKitrick, D. (1981). Generalizing from counseling analogue research on subjects' perceptions of counselor. *Journal of Counseling Psychology, 28,* 357-360.

McLemore, C. W., & Benjamin, L. S. (1979). Whatever happened to interpersonal diagnosis?: A psychosocial alternative to DSM-III. *American Psychologist, 34,* 17-34.

Matross, R. P. (1974). Socratic methods in counseling and psychotherapy. *Office for Student Affairs Research Bulletin.* University of Minnesota.

Meara, N. M. (1976). A Computer-Assisted Language Analysis System for research on natural language. In H. B. Pepinsky (Chair), *Linguistic convergence of therapist and client.* Symposium conducted at the InterAmerican Congress of Psychology, Miami Beach.

Meara, N. M. (1983, August). CALAS: Conceptualizations and caveats in communicating and counseling. Paper presented at the American Psychological Association Annual Meeting, Anaheim, CA.

Meara, N. M., Pepinsky, H. B., Shannon, J. W., & Muray, W. A. (1981). Semantic communication and expectations for counseling across three theoretical orientations. *Journal of Counseling Psychology, 28,* 110-118.

Meara, N. M., Shannon, J. W., & Pepinsky, H. B. (1979). Comparison of the stylistic complexity of the language of counselor and client across three theoretical orientations. *Journal of Counseling Psychology, 28,* 110-118.

Meichenbaum, D. & Gilmore, J. B. (1982). Resistance: From a cognitive-behavioral perspective. In P. Wachtel (Ed.), *Resistance in psychodynamic and behavioral therapies.* New York: Plenum.

Meltzoff, J., & Kornreich, M. (1970). *Research in psychotherapy.* New York: Atherton.

Merluzzi, T. V., Banikiotes, P. G., & Missbach, J. W. (1978). Perceptions of counselor characteristics: Contributions of counselor sex, experience, and disclosure level. *Journal of Counseling Psychology, 25,* 479-482.

Merluzzi, T., Merluzzi, B., & Kaul, T. (1977). Counselor race and power base: Effects of attitudes and behavior. *Journal of Counseling Psychology, 24,* 430-436.

Miller, A. G. (1970). Role of physical attractiveness in impression formation. *Psychonomic Science, 19,* 241-243.

Mitchell, K., Bozarth, J., & Krauft, C. (1977). A reappraisal of the therapeutic effectiveness of accurate empathy, nonpossessive warmth, and genuineness. In A. Gurman & A. Razin (Eds.), *Effective psychotherapy: A handbook of research.* New York: Pergamon Press.

Mueller, W. J. (1969). Patterns of behavior and their reciprocal impact in the family and in psychotherapy. *Journal of Counseling Psychology Monographs, 16* (No. 2, part 2).

Munjack, D., & Oziel, L. J. (1978). Resistance in the behavioral treatment of sexual dysfunctions. *Journal of Sex and Marital Therapy, 4,* 122-138.

Murray, E. J., & Jacobson, L. I. (1971). The nature of learning in traditional and behavioral psychotherapy. In A. E. Bergin & S. L. Garfield (Eds.), *Handbook of psychotherapy and behavior change.* New York: Wiley.

Murstein, B. E. (1972). Physical attractiveness and marital choice. *Journal of Personality and Social Psychology, 22,* 8-12.

Murstein, B. E., & Christy, P. (176). Physical attractiveness and marriage adjustment in middle-aged couples. *Journal of Personality and Social Psychology, 34,* 537-542.

Nisbett, R. E., & Wilson, T. D. (1977). Telling more than we can know: Verbal reports on mental processes. *Psychological Review, 84,* 231-259.

Olson, D., & Cromwell, R. (1975). Power in families. In R. Cromwell & D. Olson (Eds.), *Power in families.* Beverly Hills, CA: Sage.

Orlinsky, D. E., & Howard, K. I. (1978). The relation of process to outcome in psychotherapy. In A. Bergin & S. Garfield (Eds.), *Handbook of psychotherapy and behavior change* (pp. 283-330). New York: Wiley.

Patton, M. J., & Meara, N. M. (forthcoming). The analysis of natural language in psychological treatment. In R. J. Russell (Ed.), *Spoken interaction in psychotherapy: Strategies of discovery.* New York: Plenum Publishers.

Patton, M. (1969). Attraction, discrepancy, and responses to psychological treatment. *Journal of Counseling Psychology, 16,* 317-324.

Patton, M. J., Fuhriman, A. J., & Bieber, M. R. (1977). A model and metalanguage for research on psychological counseling. *Journal of Counseling Psychology, 24,* 34-35.

Patterson, G. (1982, August). *An empirical study of resistance.* Invited address at meeting of the American Psychological Association, Washington, D. C.

Pepinsky, H. B. (1974). A metalanguage for systematic research on human communication via natural language. *Journal of the American Association for Information Science, 25,* 59-69.

Pepinsky, H. B. (1985). Language and the production and interpretation of social interactions. In H. Fisher (Ed.), *Language and logic in personality and society.* NY: Columbia University Press, pp. 93-129.

Pepinsky, H. B., Baker, W. M., Matalon, R., May, G. D., & Staubus, A. M. (1977). *A user's manual for the Computer-Assisted Language Analysis System.* Columbus: The Ohio State University Group for Research and Development in Language and Social Policy.

Pepinsky, H. B., & DeStefano, J. S. (1983). Interactive discourse in the classroom as organizational behavior. In B. A. Hutson (Ed.), *Advances in reading/language research,* Greenwich: JAI Press.

Pepinsky, H. B., & Karst, T. O. (1964). Convergence: A phenomenon in counseling and psychotherapy. *American Psychologist, 19,* 333-338.

Pepinsky, H. B., & Patton, M. J. (Eds.). (1971). *The psychological experiment: A practical accomplishment.* Elmsford, NY: Pergamon.

Perls, F. S. (1969). *Gestalt therapy verbatim.* Moab, Utah: Real People Press.

Petty, R. E., & Cacioppo, J. T. (in press). The Elaboration Likelihood Model of Persuasion. *Advances in Experimental Social Psychology.*

Petty, R. E., & Cacioppo, J. T. (1984). The effects of involvement on responses to argument quantity and quality: Central and peripheral routes to persuasion. *Journal of Personality and Social Psychology, 46,* 69-81.

Petty, R. E., & Cacioppo, J. T. (1981). *Attitude and persuasion: Classic and contemporary approach (pp. 145-146).* Dubuque, IA: Wm. C. Brown.

Petty, R. E., & Cacioppo, J. T. (1979a). Effects of forewarning of persuasive intent and involvement on cognitive responses and persuasion. *Personality and Social Psychology Bulletin, 5,* 173-176.

Petty, R. E., & Cacioppo, J. T. (1979b). Issue involvement can increase or decrease persuasion by enhancing message-relevant cognitive responses. *Journal of Personality and Social Psychology, 37,* 1915-1926.

Petty, R. E., Cacioppo, J. T., & Goldman, R. (1981). Personal involvement as a determinant of argument-based persuasion. *Journal of Personality and Social Psychology, 41,* 847-855.

Petty, R. E., Cacioppo, J. T., & Heesacker, M. (1984). Central and peripheral routes to persuasion: Application to counseling. In R. P. McGlynn, J. E. Maddux, C. D. Stoltenberg, & J. H. Harvey (Eds.), *Social perception in clinical and counseling psychology.* Lubbock, TX: Texas Tech University Press.

Petty, R. E., Wells, G. L., & Brock, T. C. (1976). Distraction can enhance or reduce yielding to propaganda: Thought disruption versus effort justification. *Journal of Personality and Social Psychology, 34,* 874-884.

Ponterotto, J., & Furlong, M. (1985). Evaluating counselor effectiveness: A critical review of rating scale instruments. *Journal of Counseling Psychology, 32,* 597-616.

Raush, H. (1965). Interaction sequences. *Journal of Personality and Social Psychology, 2,* 487-499.

Raush, H. L., Dittman, A. T., & Taylor, T. J. (1959). The interpersonal behavior of children in residential treatment. *Journal of Abnormal and Social Psychology, 58,* 9-27.

Raush, H. L., Farbman, L., & Llewellyn, L. G. (1960). Person, setting and change in social interaction: II. A normal-control study. *Human Relations, 13,* 305-333.

Reed, J. R. (1983). *Linguistic evaluation.* Unpublished paper. The University of Tennessee, Knoxville.

Reed, J. R., Hector, M. A., & Meara, N. M. (1984, April). The effects of semantic and stylistic variations in language on perception of social influence characteristics in a counseling sophisticated population. In M. J. Patton (Chair), *Research on language analysis in counseling.* Session conducted at the annual meeting of the American Educational Research Association, New Orleans.

Rhine, R. J., & Severance, L. J. (1970). Ego-involvement, discrepancy, source credibility, and attitude change. *Journal of Personality and Social Psychology, 16,* 175-190.

Robyak, J. (1981). Effects of gender for methods of influence. *Journal of Counseling Psychology, 28,* 7-12.

Rohrbaugh, M., Tennen, H., Press, S., & White, L. (1981). Compliance, defiance, and therapeutic paradox: Guidelines for strategic use of paradoxical interventions. *American Journal of Orthopsychiatry, 51,* 454-467.

Rogers, R. W. (1984). Changing health related attitudes and behaviors: An interface of social and clinical psychology. In R. P. McGlynn, J. E. Maddux, C. D. Stoltenberg, & J. H. Harvey (Eds.), *Social perception in clinical and counseling psychology.* Lubbock, TX: Texas Tech University Press.

Rogers, C. R. (1957). The necessary and sufficient conditions of therapeutic personality change. *Journal of Counseling Psychology, 21,* 95-103.

Rosenfeld, P., Giacalone, R. A., & Tedeschi, J. T. (1984). Cognitive dissonance and impression management explanations for effort justification. *Personality and Social Psychology Bulletin, 10,* 394-401.

Rothmeier, R. C., & Dixon, D. N. (1980). Trustworthiness and influence: A reexamination in an extended version. *Journal of Counseling Psychology, 27,* 315-319.

Rush, J. E., Pepinsky, H. B., Landry, B. C., Meara, N. M., Strong, S. M., Valley, J. A., & Young, C. E. (1974). *A Computer-Assisted Language Analysis System.* (Computer and Information Science Research Center, OSU-CISRC-TR-74-1). Columbus: Ohio State University.

Sackett, G. (1979). The lag sequential analysis of contingency and cyclicity in behavioral interaction research. In J. Osofsky (Ed.), *Handbook of infant development.* New York: Wiley.

Scher, M. (1975). Verbal activity, sex, counselor experience, and success in counseling. *Journal of Counseling Psychology, 22,* 97-101.

Schmidt, L., & Strong, S. R. (1970). Expert and inexpert counselors. *Journal of Counseling Psychology, 17,* 115-118.

Shannon, C., & Weaver, W. (1949). *The mathematical theory of communication.* Urbana, IL: University of Illinois Press.

Shelton, J. L., & Levy, R. L. (1981). *Behavioral assignments and treatment compliance.* Champaign, IL: Research Press.

Shelton, J. L., & Ackerman, J. M. (1974). *Homework in counseling and psychotherapy.* Springfield, IL: Charles C Thomas.

Shostrom, E. L. (Producer). (1966). *Three approaches to psychotherapy [Film].* Santa Ana, CA: Psychological Films.

Siegel, J. and Sell, J. (1978). Effects of objective evidence of expertness and nonverbal behavior on counselor perceived expertness. *Journal of Counseling Psychology, 25,* 188-192.

Simons, J. A., & Helms, J. E. (1976). Influence of counselor's marital status, sex, and age of college and noncollege women's counselor preferences. *Journal of Counseling Psychology, 23,* 380-386.

Sobel, H., & O'Brien, B. (1979). Expectations for counseling success. *Journal of Counseling Psychology, 26,* 462-464.

Sternthal, B., Dholakia, R., & Leavitt, C. (1978). The persuasive effect of source credibility: Tests of cognitive response. *Journal of Consumer Research, 4,* 252-260.

Stoltenberg, C. D., Maddux, J. E., & Pace, T. (1986). Client cognitive style and counselor credibility: Effects on client endorsement of rational emotive therapy. *Cognitive Therapy and Research, 10,* 237-243.

Stoltenberg, C., & Davis, C. (in press). Career and study skills information: Who says what can alter message processing? *Journal of Clinical and Social Psychology.*

Stoltenberg, C. D., & McNeill, B. W. (1984). Effects of expertise and issue involvement on perceptions of counseling. *Journal of Social and Clinical Psychology, 2,* 314-325.

Strong, S. (1982). Emerging integrations of clinical and social psychology: A clinician's perspective. In G. Weary & H. Mirels (Eds.), *Integrations of clinical and social psychology* (pp. 181-213). New York: Oxford Press.

Strong, S. (1971). Experimental laboratory research in counseling. *Journal of Counseling Psychology, 18,* 106-110.

Strong, S. (1968). Counseling: An interpersonal influence process. *Journal of Counseling Psychology, 15,* 215-224.

Strong, S. R., & Claiborn, C. D. (1982). *Change through interaction: Social psychological processes of counseling and psychotherapy (pp. 60-64).* New York: Wiley-Interscience.

Strong, S., & Matross, R. (1973). Change processes in counseling and psychotherapy. *Journal of Counseling Psychology, 20,* 25-37.

Strong, S., Taylor, R., Bratton, J., & Loper, R. (1971). Nonverbal behavior and perceived counselor characteristics. *Journal of Counseling Psychology, 18,* 544-567.

Strong, S., & Schmidt, L. (1970). Expertness and influence in counseling. *Journal of Counseling Psychology, 17,* 81-87.

Strong, S., Wambach, C., Lopez, F., & Cooper, R. (1978). Motivational and equipping functions of interpretation in counseling. *Journal of Counseling Psychology, 26,* 98-107.

Strong, S. R., & Hills, H. I. (1984). *Interpersonal Communication Rating Scale.* Unpublished manuscript, Department of Psychology, Virginia Commonwealth University.

Strong, S. R., Hills, H. I., & Lanier, K. (1985). *Interpersonal influence strategies: Effects of self-enhancing and self-effacing behaviors.* Unpublished manuscript, Department of Psychology, Virginia Commonwealth University.

Strong, S., & DeVries, H. (1985). *Interpersonal influence strategies: Effects of critical and docile behavior.* Manuscript in preparation.

Sutton, C. S., & Dixon, D. (1983, August). Problem characteristics and treatment compliance. Presented as part of a symposium, entitled *"Resistance and treatment compliance,"* at the 1983 American Psychological Association Convention, Anaheim, CA.

Sutton, C. S., & Dixon, D. N. (1986). Resistance in parent training: A study of social influence. *Journal of Social and Clinical Psychology, 4,* 133-141.

Swenson, C. H., (1967). Psychotherapy as a special case of dyadic interaction: Some suggestions for theory and research. *Psychotherapy: Therapy Research, and Practice, 4,* 7-13.

Tedeschi, J. T., Schlenker, B. R., & Bonoma, T. V. (1971). Cognitive dissonance: Private ratiocination or public spectacle? *American Psychologist, 26,* 685-695.

Tesser, A. (1978). Self-generated attitude change. *Advances in Experimental Social Psychology, 11,* 289-338.

Tinsley, H. E. A., Workman, K. R., & Kass, R. A. (1980). Factor analysis of the domain of client expectancies about counseling. *Journal of Counseling Psychology, 27,* 561-570.

Tracey, T. J., & Ray, P. B. (1984). Stages of successful time-limited counseling: An interactional examination. *Journal of Counseling Psychology, 31,* 13-27.

Uhlenhuth, E., & Duncan, D. (1968). Subjective change in psychoneurotic outpatients with medical student therapists. II. Some determinants of change. *Archives of General Psychiatry, 18,* 532-540.

Vargas, A. M., & Borkowski, T. G. (1983). Physical attractiveness: Interactive effects of counselor and client on counseling process. *Journal of Counseling Psychology, 30,* 146-157.

Vargas, A., & Borkowski, J. (1982). Physical attractiveness and counseling skills. *Journal of Counseling Psychology, 29,* 246-255.

Wampold, B., & White, T. (1985). Research themes in counseling psychology: A cluster analysis of citations in the process and outcomes section of the *Journal of Counseling Psychology. Journal of Counseling Psychology, 32,* 123-126.

Watkins, C. E., Jr. (1982). The Self-Administered Life Style Analysis (SALSA). *Individual Psychology: The Journal of Adlerian Theory, Research and Practice, 38,* 343-352.

Watkins, C. E., Jr. (1984a). The individual psychology of Alfred Adler: Toward an Adlerian vocational theory. *Journal of Vocational Behavior, 24,* 28-47.

Watkins, C. E., Jr. (1984b). Using early recollections in career counseling. *Vocational Guidance Quarterly, 32,* 271-276.

Watzlawick, P., Beavin, J. H., & Jackson, D. D. (1967). *Pragmatics of human communication (A study of interactional patterns, pathologies, and paradoxes).* New York: Norton.

Weick, K. E., (1964). Reduction of cognitive dissonance through task enhancement and effort expenditure. *Journal of Abnormal Social Psychology, 68,* 533-539.

Wiggins, J. S. (1979). A psychological taxonomy of trait-descriptive terms: The interpersonal domain. *Journal of Personality and Social Psychology, 37,* 395-412.

Wilkins, W. (1971). Desensitization: Social and cognitive factors underlying the effectiveness of Wolpe's procedure. *Psychological Bulletin, 76,* 311-317.

Wilkins, W. (1973). Expectancy of therapeutic gain: An empirical and conceptual critique. *Journal of Consulting and Clinical Psychology, 40,* 69-77.

Wycoff, J. P., Davis, K. L., Hector, M. A., & Meara, N. M. (1982). A language analysis of empathic responding. *Journal of Counseling Psychology, 29,* 462-467.

Zamostny, K. P., Corrigan, J. D., & Eggert, M. A. (1981). Replication and extension of social influence processes in counseling: A field study. *Journal of Counseling Psychology, 28,* 481-489.

Zimbardo, P. (1960). Involvement and communication discrepancy as determinants of opinion conformity. *Journal of Abnormal and Social Psychology, 60,* 86-94.

Zimbardo, P., and Ebbeson, E. B. (1970). *Influencing attitudes and changing behavior.*
Reading, Mass: Addison-Wesley.
Zytowski, D. (1966). The study of therapy outcomes via experimental analogs: A review. *Journal of Counseling Psychology, 13,* 235-240.

AUTHOR INDEX

A

Abadie, P., 12
Abeles, N., 113
Ackerman, J., 81
Adler, A., 117, 119
Afflect, D., 72
Anchin, J., 124
Anderson, C., 76, 78, 83
Atkinson, D., 8, 9, 139, 141

B

Baeklund, F., 70
Bandura, A., 36, 71
Banikotes, P., 8, 119
Barak, A., 8, 9, 70, 90, 138, 139
Baumgarder, A., 82
Beal, D., 114
Beavin, J., 32, 33
Beck, J., 141
Beier, E., 108, 110
Begley, P., 9
Bem, D., 47
Benjamin, L., 114
Bergin, A., 9
Bernstein, A., 109
Berscheid, E., 101
Betz, N., 81
Bieber, M., 87, 91-92
Billings, M., 80, 81
Bishop, Y., 130
Bonoma, T., 47
Borkowski, J., 9, 97, 98, 99, 100, 102, 103, 104, 105
Bozarth, J., 105
Brady, S., 139
Brehm, S., 76

Brock, T., 69
Brown, M., 80
Brunson, B., 12
Burns, D., 101
Bushway, D., 79

C

Cacioppo, J., 43, 47, 48, 49, 50, 51, 52, 55, 56, 57, 59, 60, 61, 62, 63, 67, 68, 69, 141
Carskadden, G., 8
Carson, R., 124
Carter, J., 98, 102, 140, 141
Casas, J., 139
Cash, T., 9, 97, 101, 102
Chaiken, S., 68
Chatfield, C., 127, 130, 134
Christy, P., 102
Cialdini, R., 48, 56, 58
Claiborn, C., 1, 5, 6, 8, 9, 12, 34, 35, 40, 44, 45, 46, 49, 57, 58, 65, 67, 69, 70, 80, 141, 142, 143
Cohen, A., 67
Cook, W., 87, 89
Cooper, J., 5, 47, 67
Corrigan, J., 9, 13, 15, 38, 45, 46, 56, 62, 63, 75, 81, 86, 96, 124, 137, 139
Crawford, J., 141
Cromwell, R., 123, 136
Crowder, J., 25
Croyle, R., 67
Cutler, R., 23

D

Danser, D., 142
Davis, D., 13, 63

Dell, D., 8, 9, 12, 139
Derlega, V., 102
DeStefano, J., 87
DeVries, H., 23, 24, 29
Dholakia, R., 48
Dietzel, C., 113
Dinkmeyer, D., 118, 119
Dion, D., 101
Dipboye, R., 101
Dittman, A., 23
Dixon, D., 8, 13, 14, 15, 45, 46, 51, 56, 57,
     58, 62, 63, 65, 69, 70, 75, 77, 79, 80,
     81, 86, 137, 141
Dorn, F., 7, 9, 10, 11, 13, 15, 81
Duckro, P., 114
Duehn, W., 113
Duncan, D., 101

E

Eagly, A., 66, 69
Ebbeson, E., 79, 81
Eggert, M., 9, 139, 141
Endler, N., 32
Epperson, D., 81

F

Farbman, L., 23
Feldman, D., 142
Fazio, R., 47
Fenichel, O., 71
Festinger, L., 44, 95
Fienberg, S., 130
Forsyth, N., 6, 13
Forsyth, D., 6, 13
Frank, J., 31, 35, 101
French, J., 139
Fretz, B., 143
Freud, S., 38
Friedlander, M., 88
Friedman, H., 101
Furlong, M., 138
Fuhriman, A., 87, 91
G

Garfield, S., 57, 58, 64, 71, 72
Geer, C., 102
Gelso, C., 15, 140, 141
George, C., 114

Giacalone, R., 48
Gillen, B., 101
Gilmore, J., 77, 78, 83
Goldfried, M., 140
Goldman, L., 48, 51
Goldstein, A., 3, 76
Goodyear, R., 11, 12
Gottman, J., 132
Gottman, M., 8

H

Haase, R., 8
Hackman, H., 12, 141
Harkins, S., 68
Harmon, L., 139
Hector, M., 90
Heesacker, M., 3, 9, 49, 50, 51, 57, 139
Heilbrun, A., 71
Heller, K., 76
Helms, J., 102
Heppner, P., 3, 8, 9, 13, 14, 15, 45, 46, 51,
     56, 57, 62, 63, 69, 70, 75, 86, 137, 139
Highlen, P., 140, 141, 143
Hill, C., 88, 140, 141, 143
Hills, H., 19, 23, 24, 26, 29
Hobbs, N., 31, 35
Hoffman, M., 6
Hoffman-Graf, M., 102
Holland, J., 119, 130
Hovland, C., 48
Howard, K., 140
Hummel, T., 88, 125
Hurndon, C., 89, 90
Hurst, J., 102

J

Jackson, D., 32, 33
Jacobson, L., 102
Jaffe, J., 87
Jahn, D., 76
Janis, I., 48, 79, 80, 81, 82, 141
Jennings, R., 13
Jereb, R., 9

K

Karst, T., 87, 93
Kass, R., 70

Kaul, T., 11, 119
Kelley, J., 48
Kehr, J., 9, 102
Kerr, B., 8, 9, 38, 65, 70, 80, 102, 140, 142
Kleinke, C., 119
Kornreich, M., 71
Krauft, C., 105
Krauskopf, C., 82

L

LaCrosse, M., 8, 9, 70, 90, 138
Langs, R., 75
Lanier, K., 23, 24, 29
Latane, B., 67
Leary, T., 19, 23, 25, 26
Leavitt, C., 48
Lennard, H., 109
Levy, L., 35, 71, 77, 80, 81
Lewis, K., 9, 13, 98, 101, 102
Lemon, R., 130
Lichstein, K., 76
Lichtenberg, J., 88, 125
Llewellyn, L., 23
Lochman, J., 80
Lopez, F., 5
Losey, G., 134
Luborsky, L., 72
Lundwall, L., 70

M

McGown, D., 9
McGuire, W., 66
McKitrick, D., 139
McLemore, C., 114
McNeill, B., 56, 57, 62
Maddux, J., 60
Magnusson, D., 32
Maguire, 66
Mandracchia, S., 82
Mann, L., 79, 80, 81, 141
Matross, R., 10, 31, 36, 37, 38, 69, 75, 77, 124
Meara, N., 86, 87, 88, 89, 100, 101, 102
Meichenbaum, D., 77, 83
Meltzoff, J., 71
Menne, J., 137

Merluzzi, T., 8, 9, 11, 13, 119
Miller, A., 101
Missbach, J., 8, 119
Mitchell, K., 105
Mueller, W., 26, 30, 108
Murray, E., 102
Munjack, D., 77
Murstein, B., 102

N

Nisbett, R., 140

O

O'Brien, B., 13
Olson, D., 123, 136
Orlinsky, D., 140
Oziel, L., 77

P

Pace, T., 60
Patkin, J., 8, 9, 139
Patterson, G., 76, 84
Patton, M., 8, 86, 87, 89, 91, 92
Pepinsky, H., 86, 87, 89, 90, 91, 92
Perls, F., 39
Petty, R., 43, 47, 48, 49, 50, 51, 52, 55, 56, 57, 59, 60, 63, 67, 68, 69, 141
Pew, S., 8
Pew, W., 118
Phillips, S., 88
Ponterotto, J., 138
Press, S., 81
Proctor, E., 113

R

Raush, H., 23, 124
Raven, B., 139
Ray, P., 113
Reed, J., 89, 90
Rhine, R., 67
Robyak, J., 11, 12
Rogers, M., 3, 58
Rogers, C., 97, 104, 118
Rohrbaugh, M., 81
Rosenberg, J., 137
Rosenfeld, P., 48

Rothmeier, R., 8, 46
Rush, J., 86

S

Sackett, G., 130, 132
Scher, M., 102
Schmidt, L., 8, 9, 90, 119
Sechrest, L., 76
Sell, J., 8
Severance, L., 67
Shannon, C., 133
Shelton, J., 77, 80, 81
Shostrom, E., 92
Shullman, S., 81
Siegel, J., 8
Simons, J., 101
Sobel, H., 13
Sternthal, B., 48
Stewart, S., 76, 78, 83
Stoltenberg, C., 56, 57, 60, 62, 63
Strong, S., 1, 3, 4, 5, 6, 8, 10, 13, 14, 19, 23, 24, 26, 29, 31, 34, 37, 38, 40, 43, 44, 45, 46, 49, 52, 53, 62, 65, 67, 69, 75, 76, 77, 86, 90, 95, 96, 103, 104, 118, 124, 137, 138, 139, 141, 142, 143
Sutton, C., 80
Swensen, C., 23

T

Taylor, T., 23
Tedeschi, J., 48
Teglasi, H., 6
Tennen, H., 81
Tesser, A., 52
Tinsley, H., 70
Tracey, T., 113
Tully, T., 119

U

Uhlenhuth, E., 101

V

Vargas, A., 9, 97, 98, 99, 100, 102, 103, 104, 105

W

Walker, B., 13
Walsh, W., 9, 98, 101, 102
Walster, E., 101
Wambach, C., 5
Wampold, B., 9
Ward, S., 6, 141
Warman, R., 82
Watkins, C., 117, 119, 120
Watzlawick, P., 32, 33
Weaver, W., 133
Weick, K., 67
Wells, G., 69
White, T., 81
Wiggins, J., 19
Wilkins, W., 101
Wilson, T., 140
Wise, B., 9
Workman, K., 70
Wycoff, J., 91
Wyman, E., 90

Z

Zamostny, K., 9, 139
Zanna, M., 47
Zimbardo, P., 7, 79, 81
Zytowski, D., 14

SUBJECT INDEX

A

Attitude change, 3, 4
Attribution, 3

C

Client characteristics, 13, 66
 locus of control, 6-7
 physical attractiveness, 99-100
Client variables
 resistance, 10, 37
Cognitive dissonance, 7
Counselor Rating Form, 9
Counselor
 expertness, 8
 physical attractiveness, 8, 95
 social power, 10
 trustworthiness, 8

D

Dependence
 first order, 126
 second order, 125
 third order, 126

E

Elaboration Likelihood Model, 49
 counseling applications, 55-56

I

Interactional Psychology
 defined, 32
Interpersonal behaviors
 classification of, 20
 contingencies of, 26
 the interpretation of, 28

two levels of, 32-33
research on, 23
utility of, 21
Interpersonal influence
 principles of, 17-19
 relationship level, 36-38
Interpretation, 5
 client response to, 7
 discrepancy of, 6

L

Levels of influence, 34

P

Persuasion
 central route, 50
 peripheral route, 50

R

Reciprocal causality, 32
Research guidelines, 14
Resistance, 75-76
 types of, 77

S

Social Influence Theory
 Adlerian Theory, 117
 as a process, 124
 language patterns, 87
 language use, 86
 purpose of, 32
 review of research, 43-47
 stages of, 108
Social interaction
 characteristics of, 124
Social power bases, 11

165